How to Navigate the Extraordinary
"DAYS OF YOUR YOUTH"

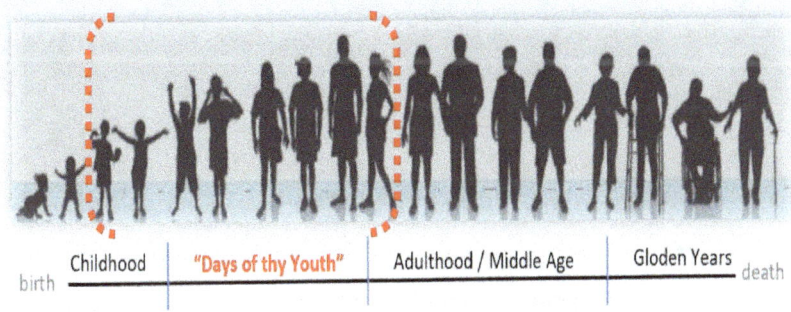

birth — Childhood | "Days of thy Youth" | Adulthood / Middle Age | Gloden Years — death

"This time in a young person's life will be like no other time in their entire lifespan. This reference book will serve as a roadmap of information and a compass to direct youth navigating this incredible period; and it will help them maximize their astounding potential while minimizing serious risks along their life's journey."

Michael A. Angelle Sr

Michael A. Angelle Sr.
How to Navigate the Extraordinary "Days of Your Youth"
All rights reserved
Copyright © 2024 by **Michael A. Angelle Sr.**

No part of this publication may be reproduced, distributed, or transmitted in any form or by any means, including photocopying, recording, or other electronic or mechanical methods, without the prior written permission of the publisher, except in the case of brief quotations embodied in critical reviews and certain other noncommercial uses permitted by copyright law.

Published by Spines Publishing Platform
ISBN: 979-8-89569-064-2

FOREWORD

Pastor Justin Jackson

Bro. Angelle is the epitome of a true Apostolic Christian...a man whose zeal and passion are revealed in his everyday life of giving all to the kingdom of God. This book comes as no surprise. As his pastor, I am privileged to see his desire to find, build young people, and teach them the wonderful ways of God. Showing a relentless effort and compassion for their cause.

This book is a must read for all who desire to know more and understand what young people are going through daily and the many reasons they struggle with the growing pains of life in general and also spiritual growth.

The book is a harmony of both biblical principles and studies conducted on the development of the brain, giving us a better grasp of what all can do to both improve and help others.

Sincerely,
Pastor Jackson

DEDICATION

Michael A. Angelle Sr.

I am honored to dedicate this book to children and young people every-where. The Bible, the Word of God, declares that children are a heritage or gift of the Lord. Children and young people are indeed a blessing from God. Furthermore, the Bible characterizes children as arrows in the hands of a mighty man. So are children in the hands of the mighty God.

How do you describe potential that is so powerful it defies words? That is the potential of every child and young person to do good. Every parent, teacher, counselor, pastor, and youth leader, plays a crucial role in nurtur-ing this potential, in recognizing and tapping into the explosive potential for good in a child or young person. I believe this is why Jesus says, "Let the children come to me and do not stop them, for the Kingdom of heaven belongs to such as these."

I dedicate this book to you, young person, to your success and achieve-ments for the cause of good and God.

Sincerely,
Michael A. Angelle Sr.

Table of Contents

Foreword by Pastor Justin Jackson	2
Dedication	3
Table of Contents	4
Introduction	6
You Are Here	9
Your Brain During the Days of Your Youth	11
Guardrails Given You by God	13
God's Expectations for the Days of Your Youth	22
Your Response	27
Your Golden Years of Learning	29
Your First 31 Days to Wisdom	31
The Book of Proverbs: Day 1 thru Day 31	33
Prayer and the Days of Your Youth	120
Protocols of Prayer	122
Elements of Prayer	129
20 Days to Prayer Life	140
Bible Reading Plan	193
Acknowledgements	195

Introduction

You, young person, are loved. You are respected and admired greatly. Let there never be a doubt in your mind regarding the fact of God's unconditional love for you, as well as the love of those whom God has placed in your life, especially your parents or guardians, your pastor, and the members of your church - the Body of Christ.

This book is one small demonstration or expression of that love as it is written, in its entirety, with you in mind. You are the singular inspiration and motivation for this book, and its content regards your happiness, well-being, future, and success in living for (and serving) Almighty God.

This is your book! Let it speak to you. Take its content personally. Its facts will enlighten you, and perhaps you will even be surprised by some of them. This book will help you establish precious and life-changing habits such as prayer and bible study. Read its pages repeatedly until you feel you have understood its message. Use its information as your roadmap, and it will guide you safely through the extraordinary and incredible days of your youth.

There will never be another time in your entire lifespan equal to this extraordinary and distinct time of your life, referred to in the Bible as **"the days of your youth."** (see Bible reference below)

Remember now thy Creator **in the days of thy youth**, while the evil days come not, nor the years draw nigh, when thou shalt say, I have no pleasure in them; (<u>**Ecclesiastes 12:1**</u>)	So remember your creator **while you are young**, before the evil days come, and the years approach when you will say, They no longer give me pleasure (<u>**Ecclesiastes 12:1**</u>)

Your youth, the period between the ages of 12 and 25, is a unique and special time. This book is specifically designed to address and uplift your age group and recognize the significance of this phase of your life. As **Ecclesiastes 12:1**, above, demonstrates, God speaks to your age group directly. The Bible uses the word youth 71 times! God designed youth to be an extraordinary and distinct time of life.

If we were to survey the outstanding biblical characters, we would find many of them were in the days of their youth when first referenced in the bible (for example: Joseph, David, Samuel, Issac, Jacob, Joshua, Rebekah, Hannah, Mary, Ruth, Daniel, Elisha, Gideon, Esther, and Josiah were all youth!). God cares about you, young person, and is very interested in your development during your youth. God even has certain and specific expectations of you during this phase of your life. Why? Because this is the phase of your life when you seriously begin to build the foundation on which the rest of your life will depend. That is of utmost importance to God and should also be for you.

This book will help you gain knowledge and understanding of God's expectations for you during your youth. You will also gain self-knowledge and an understanding of how your mind and body develop during this stage of your life. You need to know what is happening inside your mind during this time to take full advantage of some of the tremendous once-in-a-lifetime opportunities your youth offers.

Lastly, you will receive honest and respectful knowledge of your cognitive (thinking or reasoning) limitations and the associated risks that threaten to derail the days of your youth. Such knowledge will help you accept the guardrails God has placed in your life to alleviate the risks to your success and well-being.

The significance of this time in your life is truly indescribable. This is the only time in your life that you will neither be a child nor an adult. You are now an adolescent in the days of your youth. This time of your life will be like no other! A time of your life that is rich with opportunities and challenges alike.

"I wish I knew then (as a youth) what I know now (as an adult)" is a heartfelt statement often made by reminiscing adults regarding their youth experience. It acknowledges how unique and enormously consequential this phase of life is. Given the opportunity, every adult would love to return and do things better in their youth. Unfortunately, that specific phase of life has passed for adults. But for you, young person, that time or phase of life (youth) is currently at hand. You have a tremendous opportunity right now to excel in God.

This book is a tool that will empower you, as a young person, to make informed choices during your youth. Understanding and following God's expectations can prevent any regret as an adult. This book aims to equip you with the knowledge and wisdom to make your future a testament to your spiritually - responsible choices and actions today.

"**I have been young**, **and now am old; yet have I not seen the righteous forsaken, nor his seed begging bread.** (**Psalms 37:25**)

"**I have been young; now I am old; yet not once have I seen the righteous abandoned or his descendants begging for bread.** " (**Psalms 37:25**)

This book will broaden your horizons and increase your range of knowledge and perception, allowing you to see where you are on this life's journey and how you can excel living for God.

You Are Here

Imagine going to a vast, unfamiliar shopping mall in a foreign country with hundreds of stores and shops. You would likely feel lost and need help determining which way to go. You could wander around the mall and become familiar only by luck or locating the mall's map kiosk. The best option would be to find the map. You would first look for the "**YOU ARE HERE**" icon on the map. This information regarding your current location would put you at ease and give you the confidence to navigate this large and unfamiliar place. Now, you can plan your route through the mall, locate the restrooms, and find specific stores and restaurants you would like to visit. Your mall experience would be much better this way rather than wandering.

So, navigating the days of your youth is a bit like finding your way around a vast, unfamiliar mall. Many young people wander through this amazing phase of their lives, missing out on great opportunities. But what if you had a map? What if you knew exactly where you were on this life journey? You could seize every opportunity and plan the best route through these days of your youth. Knowing where you are and where you're going is always better. Right? So, let's talk about where you are right now.

From birth to about 11 years old, childhood is the first phase of your life journey. It may now appear a blur, as those years seemingly went by so fast. Everything was done for you by your parents or guardians during your childhood. They fed, bathed, clothed, and wonderfully cared for you. They ensured you were prepared for school, went to bed on time, etc. As you grew older and were more able, you began doing some of these things yourself. Your childhood needs were all met, and you were kept safe from harm or danger. Everything went according to plan. That was your childhood phase of life.

Now, you've stepped into a new chapter of life, the days of your youth, a time that's unique and full of wonder. Your mind and body are on a thrilling journey of growth and change! If you haven't noticed these changes, don't worry; they're just around the corner. It's time to marvel at God's miraculous creation of your mind and body. As the psalmist beautifully put it, 'I am fearfully and wonderfully made' **Psalms 139:14.**

When you were born, you were like a mini adult, with all the main organs an adult has (like skin, brain, heart, lungs, liver, etc.). You also had all the brain cells and hormones an adult has, but some of these hormones were sleeping in your body, waiting for the right time to wake up. Your brain cells need time to make connections and become useful. Nevertheless, your mind and body grew and changed throughout childhood.

Now, your rate of growth and maturity has begun to increase exponentially (rapidly). This is called a growth spurt. This happens because God has purposed that part of your brain called the hypothalamus will, only at the right time biologically, signal for the release of a hormone called gonadotropin. Gonadotropin then stimulates your pituitary gland, causing a chain reaction that activates your once-dormant sex hormones (testosterone - in males and estrogen/progesterone - in females). As this happens, your mind and body begin to mature sexually as an adult, which is called the onset of puberty. You will all experience some physical growth in either height and weight or both during this time. Other significant changes will occur in your body as well. For example, boys typically begin to grow facial hair, and their voices deepen; girls will see changes in their bodies, suggesting they are preparing to, one day, become mothers. These life milestones are like the map icon stating, **"YOU ARE HERE."** You have officially entered the days of your youth! It is a fascinating time in your life, and much more is happening than the physical changes we have discussed thus far. Now, please take a deep breath and let it out. God will help you excel through this most crucial phase of your life!

Your Brain Development

During your youth, your brain undergoes the most significant changes compared to any other body part. At birth, you already possess all the brain cells (neurons-grey matter) you will ever need, over 100 billion neurons. However, you cannot utilize all these brain cells yet, as the synapses and neurotransmitters (white matter) that connect these brain cells with different parts or hemispheres of your brain are still developing. This process takes years, so your understanding and ability as a child are limited.

And because of the time required for you to develop cognitively (thinking and reasoning), God purposed that you would be born into the protection of a family, with parents or guardians who would care for you, until your brain would have developed sufficiently. Now, as you enter the days of your youth, your brain is no longer that of a child's, but neither is your brain that of an adult. Your brain is currently transitioning between these two phases, and is called adolescence. Your adolescent brain is undergoing a massive renovation and is an incredible work in progress!

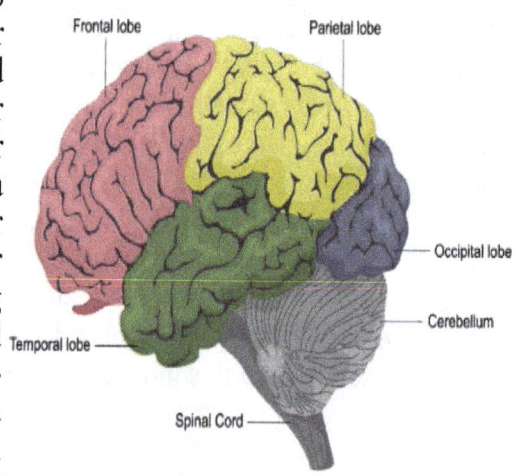

Your current brain development holds immense potential, allowing you to function at a much higher level than you could in your childhood.

The human brain is a marvel, the most impressive and complex object in the universe. To aid our discussion, we will refer to the accompanying brain image (above). Your brain develops by forming connections with synapses and neurotransmitters, starting from the back and moving towards the front. The motor and sensory areas at the back and bottom of your brain are the first to develop. The cerebellum, responsible for regulating your vision, hearing, balance and coordination, touch, and sense of space, is next. The hypothalamus, part of the parietal lobe, maintains your body functions, including hunger, thirst, sex, and aggression.

The frontal lobe, located at the front of your brain, is the executive part responsible for critical functions such as decision-making, risk assessment, judgment, abstraction, planning, self-awareness, insight, and impulse control. It's important to note that the frontal lobe is the last part of your brain to fully develop, which poses your most significant risk in the days of your youth. We will delve into your frontal lobe in detail, as it's crucial for you to understand your limitations in this respect and how God intends to mitigate this risk.

The hippocampus is located underneath your temporal lobe and encodes information and memory. This is where your most incredible opportunity and potential exist, as your hippocampus is currently supercharged and primed for learning! No other time in your life span will present this opportunity. Now is the most favorable time to learn about God and from God through reading the Bible, hearing bible preaching, and teaching. The days of your youth are your golden years for learning! The urgency and significance of this message cannot be overstated. God designed your teachability to be the hallmark of the days of your youth. You can learn anything exceptionally well during this time in your life (both good and, unfortunately, bad). What you expose your mind to and learn during this phase of your life will stick with you throughout your life! Therefore, you must make God's Word a foundation in your learning.

When the Bible refers to the heart, it is not referring to the heart muscle that pumps blood throughout the human body; it is referring to the human brain or mind, the seat of your intellect and emotions (See scripture below).

> **Keep thy heart with all diligence; for out of it are the issues of life. (Proverbs 4:23)**
>
> **Be careful how you think; your life is shaped by your thoughts. (Proverb 4:23)**

Guard and protect your mind from sin and perversion that poses as fun and entertainment on social media platforms like Facebook, YouTube, WhatsApp, Instagram, TikTok, Snapchat, and others.

> **For out of the heart proceed evil thoughts, murders, adulteries, fornication, thefts, false witness, blasphemies. (Matthew 15:19)**
>
> **For from your heart come the evil ideas which lead you to kill, commit adultery, and do other immoral things; to rob, lie, and slander others. (Matthew 15:19)**

Guardrails given to you by God

Guardrails were invented to minimize the risk of severe injury or death by providing a solid protective barrier between human lives and potentially life-threatening hazards. In the context of your life, your parents and guardians serve as these guardrails, protecting you from harm and danger. Since their invention, guardrails have saved countless lives and prevented numerous injuries. They work by deflecting errant vehicles back to the road (the safe path) or slowing an errant vehicle down and lessening the severity of a crash. Similarly, your parents and guardians guide you back to the safe path and reduce the severity of life's challenges. Their sole purpose is to protect life and limb, just as your parents and guardians protect and care for you.

Your most significant risk currently during the days of your youth will be your inability, at times, to assess risks and make critical judgments. There is no fault or shame on your part for the failure. It is just a natural part of the way the human brain develops. The part of your brain responsible for your executive decision-making, risk assessment, judgment, abstraction, planning, self-awareness, insight, and impulse control is also the last part to develop fully. Thus, there is a considerable gap or risk. However, God, who created you, has mitigated your risk by putting strong and solid guardrails in your life to protect and keep you safe until your frontal lobe is fully developed and ready to do its job.

What would happen if a child were born into this world and left without parents or guardians? That child would be completely helpless with no one to feed it, clothe it, love it, protect it, and it would not survive on its own. Thank God, that is not reality. But God designed it so that every child is born into the protection of a family and given parents or guardians to ensure that that new and precious life has everything it needs to survive and grow in a loving environment.

Guardrail #1: Parents or guardians. During your childhood phase, God gave parents or guardians to be your caregivers and protectors. They are your life's first and most essential guardians, providing you with the necessary care and protection. As you grow, they continue to serve you in a slightly different role as guardrails of protection during the days of your youth. You can now care for yourself in many respects, but you will need the special protection your parents or guardians provide for some years to come. And if you honor and respect your parents or guardians, you will be protected. You should sleep well at night knowing your parents or guardians are keeping you safe from harm or danger and have your best interest in their hearts. You should also know and understand that honoring your parents is not optional. It is a direct commandment that God expects you to obey. (see Bible references below).

My son, hear the instruction of thy father, and forsake not the law of thy mother: (**Proverbs 1:8**)	My son, heed the discipline of your father, and do not abandon the teaching of your mother; (**Proverbs 1:8**)
Honour thy father and mother; which is the first commandment with promise; 3 That it may be well with thee, and thou mayest live long on the earth. (**Ephesians 6:2-3**)	Respect your father and mother is the first commandment that has a promise added: 3 so that all may go well with you, and you may live a long time in the land. (**Ephesians 6:2-3**)

Interestingly, the commandment to honor your father and mother is the first commandment with a promise of longevity of life. God, it appears, in giving this promise, is also offering an implied warning of the potential consequences of dishonoring or disrespecting your parents, which, by implication, is a shortened life span. What a sobering thought! Yet it makes sense when considering the protective function of the parent or guardian. Remove the guardrails of parental authority and care, and consequences will follow.

Only God knows how many young people have rebelled against their parents or guardians to engage in risky behaviors that have cost them their lives or limbs as a result. The lucky ones may survive severe injury or death but are typically scarred mentally and emotionally.

Risk-taking and emotional thrill-seeking combined with the lack of risk assessment are dangerous vulnerabilities all youths share. Parents or guardians are God's answer to keep youths safe during this time of their lives. When looking back on the days of their youth, many adults will thank their parents for what they only now understand was the challenging task of keeping them safe. Guardrails endure significant impacts on themselves to serve their purpose of protecting lives and limbs. Your parents or guardians will do the same for you.

All young people experience the temptation to rebel or dismiss the guidance of their parents or guardians. It would be best if you resisted this temptation. During this phase of your life, you are expected to desire and seek independence. However, there are right and wrong ways to obtain independence. The right way is to remain respectful and obedient to your parents or guardians as the independence you crave unfolds naturally like a beautiful rose. The wrong way is to become dismissive or unruly to your parents or guardians, demanding and taking independence forcefully. Forcing a rose to open prematurely will destroy its natural beauty and fragrance.

Resist the temptation to dismiss your parents or guardians as old fogy or not as astute as you are because of your incredible ability to learn at this stage in your life. It would only negate this God-given ability. Be humble and obedient to your parents and guardians always. The quote below demonstrates a typical youthful but wrong attitude toward one's parents.

"When I was a boy of fourteen (years old), my father was so ignorant I could hardly stand to have the old man around. But when I got to be twenty-one, I was astonished by how much he'd learned in seven years." Mark Twain

The quote is a brilliant piece of irony, using words to express the opposite of their literal meaning. Therefore, what the fourteen-year-old says of his father's knowledge is true only of himself. However, the youthful lack of self-awareness rings true. Let this never be your attitude towards your parents or guardians.

We have only one passage of scripture in the bible that gives us a glimpse of Jesus Christ in the days of his youth at 12 years old. (see Bible passage below)

> And **when he was twelve years old**, they went up to Jerusalem after the custom of the feast. 43 And when they had fulfilled the days, as they returned, **the child Jesus** tarried behind in Jerusalem; and Joseph and his mother knew not of it. 44 But they, supposing him to have been in the company, went a day's journey; and they sought him among their kinsfolk and acquaintance. 45 And when they found him not, they turned back again to Jerusalem, seeking him. 46 And it came to pass, that after three days they found him in the temple, sitting in the midst of the doctors, both hearing them, and asking them questions. 47 And all that heard him were astonished at his understanding and answers. 48 And when they saw him, they were amazed: and his mother said unto him, Son, why hast thou thus dealt with us? behold, thy father and I have sought thee sorrowing. 49 And he said unto them, How is it that ye sought me? wist ye not that I must be about my Father's business? 50 And they understood not the saying which he spake unto them. 51 **And he went down with them, and came to Nazareth, <u>and was subject unto them</u>:** but his mother kept all these sayings in her heart. (<u>Luke 2:42-51</u>)

This passage of scripture demonstrates Jesus' natural development during the days of his youth. As a 12-year-old, Jesus entered the golden years of his learning. He exhibited phenomenal memory and recall of the scripture, so much so that the teachers of the Law were astonished at his understanding and answers. However, staying behind in Jerusalem, unbeknown to his parents, demonstrates the lack of judgment that we can safely attribute to the underdeveloped frontal lobe of a 12-year-old. Jesus' parents were very distraught when they discovered he was missing from the caravan, and it took them three days to get back to Jerusalem, where they found the young Jesus in the Temple.

The conclusion of this portrayal of a 12-year-old Jesus states, "he (Jesus) went down with them (his parents), and came to Nazareth, and was subject unto them." We are fortunate to have the Bible give us this glimpse of Jesus in the days of his youth! With everything we know about youth development, we can say that Jesus developed like any other youth and left a great example of what he expects every young person to do during the days of their youth.

Through this scripture passage, we witness the inherent risks of youth as seen in Jesus' life, but we also see the protective measures God has put in place. The responsibility to obey always lies with the youth, and Jesus willingly submitted to his parents' authority. You, too, can and should follow his example. Let Jesus' life inspire you to honor your parents or guardians, a crucial aspect of your journey into adulthood.

Guardrail #2: Pastor (shepherd, leader).

God gave you a pastor to help you navigate the days of your youth from a spiritual perspective. Your pastor has an anointing of God that allows him to identify future risks, dangers, or hazards to your spiritual well-being and happiness. If you pay careful attention as your pastor ministers, you will observe this profound ability in the man of God. This should build your trust in your pastor and strike fear in your heart of ever disregarding or dismissing the words or advice of your pastor. You should know and appreciate that your spiritual well-being is front and center in your pastor's heart. Your pastor takes his responsibility to help you navigate these days of your youth very seriously, and you must reciprocate by allowing your pastor to rule or govern (in) your life spiritually. Your pastor is another layer of protection given to you by God.

And **I will give you** pastors **according to mine heart, which shall feed you with knowledge and understanding.** (Jeremiah 3:15)	I will give you shepherds after my own heart, and they will feed you with knowledge and understanding. (Jeremiah 3:15)
Obey **them that have the rule over you,** and submit yourselves**: for they** watch for your souls**, as they that must** give account**, that they may do it with** joy**, and not with** grief**: for that is** unprofitable for you**.** (Hebrews 13:17)	Obey your leaders and follow their orders. They watch over your souls without resting, since they must give to God an account of their service. If you obey them, they will do their work gladly; if not, they will do it with sadness, and that would be of no help to you. (Hebrews 13:17)

Your pastor is a manifestation of God's love and care for you. God expects you to obey and submit to your pastor's authority. As **Hebrews 13:17** states, it is unprofitable to do otherwise. Disobeying your pastor can lead to serious spiritual harm. Your pastor is not just a figure of authority but a spiritual guide who can lead you to a deeper understanding of God's plan for your life.

The Bible tells us of Gehazi, a young man who defied his pastor, the prophet Elisha (**2 Kings 5**). Gehazi, after witnessing the miraculous healing of Naaman, the Syrian, from an incurable disease called leprosy, chose to seek and accept (worldly) gifts that his pastor, Elisha, had taught him to reject. The consequences were severe. Elisha, speaking on behalf of God, pronounced judgment. Gehazi, who had the potential to follow in the footsteps of Elisha and become a great prophet, instead became an incurable leper. His disobedience led to a tragic outcome and a missed opportunity. Your hopes and dreams are not of becoming a failure. You want to greatly succeed in all that you do. God will help you.

> But he went in, and stood before his master. And Elisha said unto him, Whence comest thou, Gehazi? And he said, Thy servant went no whither. 26 And he said unto him, Went not mine heart with thee, when the man turned again from his chariot to meet thee? Is it a time to receive money, and to receive garments, and oliveyards, and vineyards, and sheep, and oxen, and menservants, and maidservants? 27 The leprosy therefore of Naaman shall cleave unto thee, and unto thy seed for ever. And he went out from his presence a leper as white as snow. (**2 Kings 5:25-27**)

The protections God put in our lives will do us no good if we don't honor and respect them. All the brokenhearted man of God, Elisha, could do was lament, "**Went not my heart with thee.**" The example of your pastor alone should be enough to deter you from doing the wrong things. Yet, it depends on how you understand and regard what God has placed in your life. (i.e., your parents, your pastor, your church)

A similar tragedy is found in **1 Samuel 15**, which recounts the story of King Saul and his pastor, the prophet Samuel. When King Saul rebels and disobeys a direct command of the man of God, the Bible says his pastor, Samuel, "cried unto the Lord all night" on his behalf. However, Saul's disobedience to his pastor had sealed his doom. And God rejected his kingship. (see Bible reference below)

> For rebellion is as the sin of witchcraft, and stubbornness is as iniquity and idolatry. Because thou hast rejected the word of the Lord, he hath also rejected thee from being king. (1 Samuel 15:23)

> Rebellion against him is as bad as witchcraft, and arrogance is as sinful as idolatry. Because you rejected the Lord's command, he has rejected you as king. (1 Samuel 15:23)

Your pastor is your second layer of protection. This guardrail is different in that it has a more significant spiritual implication. Your parents or guardians watch for your safety and well-being, and your pastor watches for your soul! You are very precious to the man of God in your life. Don't be afraid to communicate with your pastor. Please share your thoughts with him and ask for his advice. Allow him to help guide you during the days of your youth. Above all, stay submitted and obedient to your pastor.

Again, your pastor is like the gardener in the scripture passage below. He will do everything he can as a pastor to help you, lead you, and guide you through the days of your youth. You must cooperate with your man of God if you are to succeed. It may be that the only thing between you and disaster is the prayers of your pastor on your behalf as the gardener below pleaded for the life of that fig tree. (See scripture below)

> He spake also this parable; A certain man had a fig tree planted in his vineyard; and he came and sought fruit thereon, and found none. 7 Then said he unto the dresser of his vineyard, Behold, these three years I come seeking fruit on this fig tree, and find none: cut it down; why cumbereth it the ground? 8 And he answering said unto him, Lord, let it alone this year also, till I shall dig about it, and dung it: 9 And if it bear fruit, well: and if not, then after that thou shalt cut it down. (Luke 13:6-9)

> Then Jesus told them this parable: There was once a man who had a fig tree growing in his vineyard. He went looking for figs on it but found none. 7 So he said to his gardener, 'Look, for three years I have been coming here looking for figs on this fig tree, and I haven't found any. Cut it down! Why should it go on using up the soil?' 8 But the gardener answered, 'Leave it alone, sir, just one more year; I will dig around it and put in some fertilizer. 9 Then if the tree bears figs next year, so much the better; if not, then you can have it cut down. (Luke 13:6-9)

Guardrail #3: the Church (ekklesia– called out ones).

The Church is the third layer of protection or guardrail that God has placed in your life. God has given you the privilege to be a part of the greatest (spiritual) organism on earth, the church, which is His body. The church will supply your needs in a wholesome and godly environment. It's a safe place, especially during the days of your youth. But its most unique role is in providing spiritual nourishment found nowhere else. All that is godly, wholesome, and spiritual is part of the function of the church.

The church is God's spiritual dwelling place. When we receive the Holy Ghost baptism, as recorded in the book of **Acts 2:38-39**, we become partakers of God's divine nature and genuinely part of His body. God's presence within each member of the body is what makes the church great. When the church members assemble themselves in the sanctuary, the power and presence of God are magnified. The following scripture passages describe the church as a body in terms of its unity and as a building or temple, describing its function as a dwelling place of God.

For as the body is one, and hath many members, and all the members of that one body, being many, are one body: so also is Christ. 13 For by one Spirit are we all baptized into one body, whether we be Jews or Gentiles, whether we be bond or free; and have been all made to drink into one Spirit. (1 Corinthians 12:12-13)	For just as the body is one but has many parts; and all the parts of the body, though many, constitute one body; so it is with the Messiah. 13 For it was by one Spirit that we were all immersed into one body, whether Jews or Gentiles, slaves or free; and we were all given the one Spirit to drink. (1 Corinthians 12:12-13)
And are built upon the foundation of the apostles and prophets, Jesus Christ himself being the chief corner stone; 21 In whom all the building fitly framed together groweth unto an holy temple in the Lord: 22 In whom ye also are builded together for an habitation of God through the Spirit. (Ephesians 2:20-22)	You have been built on the foundation of the apostles and the prophets, with the cornerstone being Jesus the Messiah himself. 21 In union with him the whole building is held together, and it is growing into a holy temple in union with the Lord. 22 Yes, in union with him, you yourselves are being built together into a spiritual dwelling-place for God. (Ephesians 2:20-22)

God designed the church to care for itself similarly to a human body in that its many members work together to care for the whole body. (See the Bible reference below)

> "From whom the whole body fitly joined together and compacted by that which every joint supplieth, according to the effectual working in the measure of every part, maketh increase of the body unto the edifying of itself in love." (Ephesians 2:20-22)

No youth should ever turn to the world to have their needs met. God gave you a church to supply all your needs in a spiritually wholesome and godly manner. You should participate in everything the church does (i.e., youth camps, youth rallies, youth conferences, youth trips, youth prayer, youth fellowship, youth choir, bible memory work, youth outreach, seasonal banquets, plays, etc.). The church will meet all your needs if you wholeheartedly participate in all its activities and stay mentally and spiritually engaged.

The world or society does not care for its members in the same way as the church does. The church will do everything in its power, in a godly and wholesome manner, to ensure you are saved, happy, and spiritually productive (fit for the Kingdom of God). The world will do everything and anything to keep you enslaved to sin and to your carnal human nature, making you unfit for the Kingdom of God. You must love your church.

15 Love not the world, neither the things that are in the world. If any man love the world, the love of the Father is not in him. 16 For all that is in the world, the lust of the flesh, and the lust of the eyes, and the pride of life, is not of the Father, but is of the world. (1 John 2:15-16)	15 Do not love the world or anything that belongs to the world. If you love the world, you do not love the Father. 16 Everything that belongs to the world—what the sinful self desires, what people see and want, and everything in this world that people are so proud of—none of this comes from the Father; it all comes from the world. (1 John 2:15-16)

God has given you three layers of protection: (1) parents or guardians, (2) a pastor, and (3) **the church**. You are set up for success. Yet, the responsibility for that success lies within your faith and obedience to God.

God's Expectations

God has indeed set you up for success during the days of your youth and beyond! However, that success is in your hands at this stage. Are you surprised? This is because you've naturally and biologically exited your childhood stage and have now entered the incredible days of your youth. You are now self-accountable, which balances against your astounding God-given ability and potential. This means that God, who knows you intimately, trusts and expects you to be responsible and to do the right things during the days of your youth. You will receive instructions in righteousness from the preaching and teaching of your pastor, a sign of the trust God has in you.

God knows exactly what you can accomplish, and God knows your limitations as well. God indeed expects you to use ALL your youthful vitality, God-given and explosive learning potential, talent, strength, and ability in a manner that can be offered up as a sacrifice pleasing to Himself. To do otherwise with the days of your youth would be displeasing to God. This is a fact substantiated by the Bible passage below.

> Rejoice, O young man, in thy youth; and let thy heart cheer thee in the days of thy youth, and walk in the ways of thine heart, and in the sight of thine eyes: but know thou, that for all these things God will bring thee into judgment. (Ecclesiastes 11:9)
>
> Young person, if you spend your youth only having fun, if you use your early years just to entertain yourself, if you follow your heart as you live your life, and let your eyes be your guide; understand that for all these things God will bring you to judgment. (Ecclesiastes 11:9)

Let these scriptures serve as your official notice that God has great expectations of you during your youth. You are accountable to God for the actions you take and the plans you make. This is not a time for you to live haphazardly or with youthful abandonment of self-discipline. God has better expectations of you.

Nothing is wrong with having fun, but God does not expect you to spend the days of your youth only having fun. There is nothing wrong with entertaining yourself, but God does not expect you to use the days of your youth only to entertain yourself. The expectation of God is for you to balance the time you spend with fun and entertainment with time spent growing in the knowledge of God.

God's expectation will require effort to apply self-discipline to the use of your time. You can spend too much time on activities that are only self-serving and have no spiritual value. The best-case scenario is engaging in activities you and God can enjoy together. For example, playing a video football game for hours will have no lasting or spiritual value. Still, hours practicing a musical instrument is valuable in that it strengthens your mental understanding and can be used in the worship of Almighty God. This is not to say you should not play a video football game, but to say you must severely limit your time on activities with no lasting or spiritual value. The idea is to be perfectly in balance with regard to pleasing God.

God expects the days of your youth to be well-lived in a godly and self-disciplined manner. This is because you are going somewhere great, as God has a beautiful plan for your life. The days of your youth are critical to successfully fulfilling that plan. Proper focus, time, and effort must be put towards fulfilling God's plan for your life. Balance and moderation are the keys to meeting God's expectations in your life.

> **For I know the thoughts that I think toward you, saith the Lord, thoughts of peace, and not of evil, to give you an expected end. (Jeremiah 29:11)**
>
> For I know what plans I have in mind for you,' says the Lord, 'plans for well-being, not for bad things; so that you can have hope and a future. (Jeremiah 29:11)

You must be willing to work with God to see His plan come to fruition in your life. God will strongly urge but never force you against your own will. The accountability we've discussed in this section does not mean that God is waiting to crush you as soon as you make a mistake or fail. By accountability, we mean the recognition of your ability to assume responsibility for your actions now in the days of your youth. In addition to honoring and respecting God's guardrails in your life, God expects you to mature mentally (apply self-discipline and grow up) as you depart childhood and enter adolescence. Do not be afraid of responsibility. Taking responsibility is an essential and proper part of your spiritual development, and working with God on this journey is a joy.

> When I was a child, my speech, feelings, and thinking were all those of a child; now that I am an adult, I have no more use for childish ways." (1 Corinthians 13:11)

> **The heart is deceitful above all things, and desperately wicked**: who can know it? (**Jeremiah 17:9**)

You can never know where your heart will lead you, young person. Only God knows how many youths have followed their hearts to complete misery in life. The best-case scenario is for every youth to follow the path of the Word of God, the Bible. It is, in fact, an expectation of God. God expects youth to follow the leading and biblical teaching of their pastor. Only then will you eliminate all risks of an uncertain direction.

> There is a way that seemeth right unto a man, but the end thereof are the ways of death. (**Proverbs 16:25**) What you think is the right road may lead to death. (**Proverbs 16:25**)

Neither can you, as a youth, let your eyes be your guide. Modern technology presents an endless supply of enticements for the eyes and ears via social media. On social media, there is a perverse mix of sin, triviality, sensuality, and deception disguised as fun and entertainment. The result of these influences on young minds is confusion. You are more susceptible to being easily led astray by social media influencers, because many of them are in your age group and have achieved popularity perceived by youth to indicate rightness. However, many of these influencers do not follow the path of the Word of God, the Bible. Therefore, do not allow your eyes and ears to be corrupted by social media's nonsense.

> ...**the eye is not satisfied with seeing**, **nor the ear filled with hearing**. (**Ecclesiastes 1:8**)

Modern technology is not all bad and can be used responsibly, but God has a much better way for you to navigate the days of your youth. Instead of searching the World Wide Web, you should search the scriptures! Through reading and studying God's WORD, the Bible, you will develop an internal moral compass that is more accurate than any earthly compass and will lead you on the right path. God has provided that His WORD would be a lamp and a light to guide you. You should replace any social media apps on your cell phone with Bible technology apps (such as a bible app, an audio bible app, the bible memory app, etc.). In this way, you blunt the effect of worldly influences that's attempting to destroy your walk with God.

> **Thy word is a lamp unto my feet, and a light unto my path.** **(Psalms 119:105)**
>
> **This I say then,** Walk in the Spirit, and ye shall not fulfil the lust of the flesh. **(Galatians 5:16)**

God expects you to walk in the Spirit, not in your carnal, fleshly nature. You are capable of this! With God's help, you can learn the right things to do and where to invest your time and effort. It may take time, but you have the potential to surpass God's expectations for your youth.

You have been set up for success. You have solid and protective guardrails consisting of your parents and guardians, your pastor, and your church. You have received knowledge of God's expectations of you during your youth. We have discussed your limitations and the associated risks that threaten to derail you.

We have covered a lot of good information thus far. Let it all soak in. You may even want to re-read certain sections to be sure you understand them completely. When you feel you've absorbed this knowledge, it is time to take action on what you have learned. This is where your accountability to what God expects of you during the days of your youth comes into play. You have been given actionable information. The choice of what to do with this information is yours alone. Some may decline to do anything with actionable information, but know that declining to act is as much a decision as it would be to act. God will not force you. God is a gentleman, but He will urge you to choose the right way through the preaching and teaching of your pastor and other ministry.

> **Remember now thy Creator in** the days of thy youth, **while the evil days come not, nor the years draw nigh, when thou shalt say, I have no pleasure in them;** **(Ecclesiastes 12:1)**

In this scripture, God urges you to bring all of your youthful vitality, potential, gifts, talent, strength, and abilities into the service of your Creator during your youth. All these things have been given to you by God, who created and loves you. God expects you to reciprocate His love through your faithfulness and obedience. The best time to fully engage your faith in God is in your youth!

God's joy is boundless when anyone, regardless of their past, dedicates their life to His service. But imagine the significance of serving God in the prime of your youth. You are not just part of God's plan but integral to it. Your role is not just important; it is indispensable. Isn't that a role you want to play? You are destined to do exceptionally well serving Almighty God.

You have nothing to fear. Only know that God has great expectations for your life. You are not your own. You were bought with the price of the crucifixion that Jesus Christ endured, and he shed blood on your behalf to deliver you from unrighteousness and to redeem you unto himself so that you would be zealous of good works.

In this scenario, your expectations of yourself and God's expectations of you are in alignment. This is where you want to live the days of your youth. You and God agree. Perfect!

Your response and willingness to obey what we've discussed in this book will give testament to the alignment of your and God's expectations.

| 10 Teach me to do thy will; for thou art my God: thy spirit is good; lead me into the land of uprightness. (Psalms 143:10) | 10 You are my God; teach me to do your will. Be good to me, and guide me on a safe path. (Psalms 143:10) |

Your Response

Your response to what you have learned thus far is of utmost importance. This is where you apply what you have learned to your life. This is where you take full advantage of your God-given opportunity and potential. God richly rewards faith and obedience. If you eagerly accept the responsibility to meet the expectations of God, you will achieve incredible results and gain tremendous advantages for yourself that will last a lifetime.

God has a beautiful plan for your life. The foundation of that plan is laid in earnest during your youth. You and God will build that foundation together. You will become an avid reader and doer of the WORD of God, the Bible. God has supplied everything you need to know and do to be successful in His WORD. However, you must now read the Bible differently than you have ever read it before. You must now read the Bible with an understanding that it is God's WORD for your life. Read it with great interest and anticipation, as if searching for a hidden treasure. If you take the time to read your Bible in this way, God will reciprocate by taking the time to talk to you and teach you through the Bible personally. For example, in the scripture passage below, God instructs young people to keep themselves pure. Let this be proof that God is interested in your well-being. God is speaking to you directly, young person. Taking the time to read and allowing God to talk to you is that simple yet more powerful than you can imagine, depending on your attitude towards the WORD of God and your faith.

Wherewithal shall a young man cleanse his way? by taking heed thereto according to thy word. (Psalms 119:9)	How can a young man keep his way pure? By guarding it according to your word. (Psalms 119:9)

Though the Bible looks and reads like any ordinary book, the Bible is no ordinary book. The Bible is the WORD of God. The Bible contains 66 books, letters, and over 32,000 scripture verses. Within the bible, you'll read many different literary genres such as law, prophecy, poetry, etc., and the Bible alone, of all the books in the world, has an indelible stamp of divinity. The Bible has been translated into all languages and is accessible to all. You may even have your own Bible with your name stenciled on it. However, the Bible will do you little good if you are not in awe of the God of the Bible. As a young person, you must develop a deep love and appreciation for the Bible.

The days of your youth are the most favorable time in your entire life span for reading and studying the Bible. You could not do yourself a greater disservice than to let your current golden years of learning go past without a serious and personal study of the Bible. The Bible is the only book given by God whereby you can find instructions on how you can and should fulfill your purpose for living and take advantage of every opportunity God has given you during these days of your youth. No other book comes close. No other book on earth will provide you with such an awareness of and aversion to sin. For this reason alone, the Bible is of the most significant value to you and is worthy of being read by all. Learning the Bible is like learning a new language. It is the language of God. When someone shows you much love, the response should be reciprocal. You show them much love in return. God loves you and has proven that He cares about your well-being. You should respond in kind by taking His WORD, the Bible, seriously and let the reading of the Bible be the actual groundbreaking event of the days of your youth. The following section will discuss how you learn things more efficiently, faster, and more intensely during this phase of your life. God designed it to be so. It is genuinely learned when you intentionally and eagerly learn the Bible during youth!

"Thy word have I hid in mine heart, that I might not sin against thee." (**Psalms 119:11**)

God encourages you to learn about and from Him through preaching and teaching and a personal study of His Word, the Bible. This is the challenge every young person should eagerly accept. You have nothing to lose and everything to gain by responding to God's expectations in this manner.

"Take **my yoke upon you,** and learn of me; **for I am meek and lowly in heart: and ye shall find rest unto your souls.**" (**Matthew 11:29**)

Your Golden Years of Learning

"These are the best decade of life. No age is so responsive to all the best and wisest adult endeavor. In no psychic soil, too does seed, both bad as well as good, strike such deep root, grow so rankly or bear fruit so quickly or surely" Granville Stanley Hall.

Mr. Hall, the first to earn a doctorate in psychology, spoke with excitement and amazement at the stunning ability of youth to learn. Many years of study and research have only strengthened and confirmed that your (adolescent) mind or brain at this stage is not just supercharged, but also holds immense potential for learning, offering a hopeful and optimistic outlook.

Since birth, you've been on a continuous learning journey. At the start, your brain was packed with neurons (grey matter) but lacked the necessary wiring (white matter). Now, you've reached a crucial stage where your brain's wiring is catching up with the number of neurons. Over time, your brain has developed more neural pathways for learning, with your hippocampus, the memory and information encoder, being more active and engaged than an adult's.

Learning is a process driven by excitation, which occurs when you encounter new information or experiences. This excitation triggers the brain to form more connections between neurons and synapses. The more the brain is stimulated, the more it's wired. In your youth, learning and memory are significantly more potent than in later life. This is because your adolescent brain is more receptive to excitation between brain cells, and the connections becomes much stronger. In other words, the more you revisit or relearn a piece of information, the stronger that learning pathway becomes, making it easier to recall. This is how knowledge becomes ingrained.

Another way to think about this learning process is to think about your conscious and subconscious mind. Information in the form of thoughts you reject or deem unimportant will be purged from your conscious mind (short-term memory), and thoughts you choose to keep will pass on to your subconscious mind (long-term memory). Note: You cannot control thoughts once they enter your subconscious mind. Your conscious mind will be an essential gatekeeper of your thoughts. Your subconscious will accept and retain the information you consciously allow.

Therefore, you must be extremely careful in choosing what information you expose your mind to learning. Your subconscious thoughts produce your feelings, which create your actions and the accompanying results or outcomes. Imprinted thoughts will express themselves in your habits. In other words, your life consists of the total of your thoughts. If you think right, you will live right.

In computer technology, they have an expression, "garbage in, garbage out," or GIGO, which refers to the idea that in any system, the output quality is determined by the quality of the input. The highest quality information you can ever input into your mind is the WORD of God, the Bible. The absolute best time to learn the bible is in the days of your youth! Most of your memories as an adult will be comprised of things you learned during the days of your youth. Make good memories!

Let learning the WORD of God, the Bible, be the groundbreaking event of your youth! Wouldn't it be great if you gave the bulk of your golden years of learning to learning about and from Almighty God? You could not go wrong with this approach. What you learn now in the days of your youth will become the foundation on which the rest of your life is built or constructed. To build on the WORD of God is to build on solid bedrock. It would be impossible to exaggerate the magnitude of your potential at this phase of your life. Will you seize this once-in-a-lifetime opportunity? If you answer yes, you will never regret it!

> **24 Therefore whosoever** heareth these sayings of mine, and doeth them**, I will liken him unto a wise man, which built his house upon a rock: 25 And the rain descended, and the floods came, and the winds blew, and beat upon that house;** and it fell not: for it was founded upon a rock. **(Matthew 7:24-25)**

Your First 31 Days to Wisdom

Suppose for this section that you have just entered the incredible days of your youth. You love, honor, and respect the protective guardrails God has placed in your life. You know and completely understand what God expects of you during the days of your youth. You know some of how your brain works and how incredibly you learn at this stage. You are sure that God loves you and is very much interested in this period of your life. You accept the responsibility and the challenge of meeting God's expectations. You are thrilled at the prospect of exceeding God's expectations and becoming all God would have you to become. You are happy to take advantage of this once-in-a-lifetime opportunity to use your golden years of learning to learn about and from God. You are ready, fully prepared, to set the motion to fulfill God's plan and purpose for your life. You choose voluntarily to apply the best-case scenario to this stage of your life. You anticipate your future and think, "This will be good!"

However, you don't know how or where to begin. The rest of this book will be dedicated to helping you get started acquiring the faith, knowledge, and understanding required to bring all the blessings of the days of your youth to fruition. The two most practical and essential ways for you to go about pleasing God during the day of your youth are through (1) **establishing a prayer life** and (2) **building a daily routine of reading the WORD of God, the Bible.** We'll start with reading the bible first.

As you embark on this journey of reading and enjoying the Bible, remember that we will take it one day at a time. We will read one chapter each day for the next 31 days. The following pages will contain the entire book of Proverbs, a perfect starting point. Each chapter will be referred to as a day, reinforcing the principle of daily Bible reading. Your commitment to this plan is crucial for your spiritual growth.

We have provided you with two versions of the Bible: (1) the preferred King James Version and (2) a modern English translation (a combination of Today's English Version and the Complete Jewish Bible). In this way, you will have alternate renderings of difficult-to-understand passages. Reading the Bible has never been easier.

You are now ready to start building your foundation on the bedrock of the WORD of God. Read these following pages with great interest, anticipation, and desire, knowing that the WORD of God will speak to you. You will gain wisdom these next 31 days, but this is just the beginning! You are now about to begin building a daily Bible reading routine that will, in time, become an excellent and advantageous habit. Your thoughts will become infused with the power and wisdom of the WORD of God, the Bible. Bible-influenced thoughts will produce better feelings and create better actions and results or outcomes in your life. Wow! This is so exciting! Above all, you will develop an internal moral compass and always know how to please God, your creator.

> 1 Blessed is the man that walketh not in the counsel of the ungodly, nor standeth in the way of sinners, nor sitteth in the seat of the scornful. 2 But his delight is in the law of the Lord; and in his law doth he meditate day and night. 3 And he shall be like a tree planted by the rivers of water, that bringeth forth his fruit in his season; his leaf also shall not wither; and whatsoever he doeth shall prosper. (**Psalms 1:1-3**)
>
> 1 This book of the law shall not depart out of thy mouth; but thou shalt meditate therein day and night, that thou mayest observe to do according to all that is written therein: for then thou shalt make thy way prosperous, and then thou shalt have good success. (**Joshua 1:8**)

For the next 31 consecutive days, read the following pages (the book of Proverbs), provided in two versions of the Bible. We have labeled each as a day to reinforce the idea that the Bible should be read daily. Read only one chapter per day, but feel free to re-read each day's chapter as many times as you wish. Re-reading strengthens the learning pathways for that information.

Read Read Read Read Read Read Read

If you have never read the book of Proverbs before, you are in for a treat! The book of Proverbs will raise your spiritual IQ as it touches so many subjects regarding life, morals, ethics, money, good judgment and more.

Happy groundbreaking! Take notes as you read, if you would take it up a notch. Enjoy!

Proverbs - Day 1

1 The proverbs of Solomon the son of David, king of Israel; 2 To know wisdom and instruction; to perceive the words of understanding; 3 To receive the instruction of wisdom, justice, and judgment, and equity; 4 To give subtilty to the simple, to the young man knowledge and discretion. 5 A wise man will hear, and will increase learning; and a man of understanding shall attain unto wise counsels: 6 To understand a proverb, and the interpretation; the words of the wise, and their dark sayings. 7 The fear of the Lord is the beginning of knowledge: but fools despise wisdom and instruction. 8 My son, hear the instruction of thy father, and forsake not the law of thy mother: 9 For they shall be an ornament of grace unto thy head, and chains about thy neck. 10 My son, if sinners entice thee, consent thou not. 11 If they say, Come with us, let us lay wait for blood, let us lurk privily for the innocent without cause: 12 Let us swallow them up alive as the grave; and whole, as those that go down into the pit:

1 The proverbs of Solomon the son of David, king of Israel, 2 are for learning about wisdom and discipline; for understanding words expressing deep insight; 3 for gaining an intelligently disciplined life, doing what is right, just and fair; 4 they can make an inexperienced person clever and teach young people how to be resourceful. 5 Someone who is already wise will hear and learn still more; someone who already understands will gain the ability to counsel well; 6 he will understand proverbs, obscure expressions, the sayings and riddles of the wise. 7 To have knowledge, you must first have reverence for the Lord. Fools have no respect for wisdom and refuse to learn. 8 My son, heed the discipline of your father, and do not abandon the teaching of your mother; 9 they will be a garland to grace your head, a medal of honor for your neck. 10 My son, if sinners entice you, don't go along with them. 11 Suppose they say, "Come on; let's find someone to kill! Let's attack some innocent people for the fun of it! 12 They may be alive and well when we find them, but they'll be dead when we're through with them!

13 We shall find all precious substance, we shall fill our houses with spoil: 14 Cast in thy lot among us; let us all have one purse: 15 My son, walk not thou in the way with them; refrain thy foot from their path: 16 For their feet run to evil, and make haste to shed blood. 17 Surely in vain the net is spread in the sight of any bird. 18 And they lay wait for their own blood; they lurk privily for their own lives. 19 So are the ways of every one that is greedy of gain; which taketh away the life of the owners thereof. 20 Wisdom crieth without; she uttereth her voice in the streets: 21 She crieth in the chief place of concourse, in the openings of the gates: in the city she uttereth her words, saying, 22 How long, ye simple ones, will ye love simplicity? and the scorners delight in their scorning, and fools hate knowledge? 23 Turn you at my reproof: behold, I will pour out my spirit unto you, I will make known my words unto you. 24 Because I have called, and ye refused; I have stretched out my hand, and no man regarded; 25 But ye have set at nought all my counsel, and would none of my reproof:

13 We'll find all kinds of riches and fill our houses with loot! 14 Come and join us, and we'll all share what we steal." 15 My child, don't go with people like that. Stay away from them. 16 They can't wait to do something bad. They're always ready to kill. 17 It does no good to spread a net when the bird you want to catch is watching, 18 but people like that are setting a trap for themselves, a trap in which they will die. 19 Robbery always claims the life of the robber—this is what happens to anyone who lives by violence. 20 Listen! Wisdom is calling out in the streets and marketplaces, 21 calling loudly at the city gates and wherever people come together: 22 "Foolish people! How long do you want to be foolish? How long will you enjoy making fun of knowledge? Will you never learn? 23 Listen when I reprimand you; I will give you good advice and share my knowledge with you. 24 I have been calling you, inviting you to come, but you would not listen. You paid no attention to me. 25 You have ignored all my advice and have not been willing to let me correct you.

26 I also will laugh at your calamity; I will mock when your fear cometh; 27 When your fear cometh as desolation, and your destruction cometh as a whirlwind; when distress and anguish cometh upon you. 28 Then shall they call upon me, but I will not answer; they shall seek me early, but they shall not find me: 29 For that they hated knowledge, and did not choose the fear of the Lord: 30 They would none of my counsel: they despised all my reproof. 31 Therefore shall they eat of the fruit of their own way, and be filled with their own devices. 32 For the turning away of the simple shall slay them, and the prosperity of fools shall destroy them. 33 But whoso hearkeneth unto me shall dwell safely, and shall be quiet from fear of evil. (Provers 1:1-33)

26 So when you get into trouble, I will laugh at you. I will make fun of you when terror strikes— 27 when it comes on you like a storm, bringing fierce winds of trouble, and you are in pain and misery. 28 Then you will call for wisdom, but I will not answer. You may look for me everywhere, but you will not find me. 29 You have never had any use for knowledge and have always refused to obey the Lord. 30 You have never wanted my advice or paid any attention when I corrected you. 31 So then, you will get what you deserve, and your own actions will make you sick. 32 Inexperienced people die because they reject wisdom. Foolish people are destroyed by their own lack of concern. 33 But whoever listens to me will have security. He will be safe, with no reason to be afraid." (Proverbs 1:1-33)

Proverbs - Day 2

1 My son, if thou wilt receive my words, and hide my commandments with thee; 2 So that thou incline thine ear unto wisdom, and apply thine heart to understanding; 3 Yea, if thou criest after knowledge, and liftest up thy voice for understanding; 4 If thou seekest her as silver, and searchest for her as for hid treasures; 5 Then shalt thou understand the fear of the Lord, and find the knowledge of God. 6 For the Lord giveth wisdom: out of his mouth cometh knowledge and understanding. 7 He layeth up sound wisdom for the righteous: he is a buckler to them that walk uprightly. 8 He keepeth the paths of judgment, and preserveth the way of his saints. 9 Then shalt thou understand righteousness, and judgment, and equity; yea, every good path. 10 When wisdom entereth into thine heart, and knowledge is pleasant unto thy soul; 11 Discretion shall preserve thee, understanding shall keep thee: 12 To deliver thee from the way of the evil man, from the man that speaketh froward things; 13 Who leave the paths of uprightness, to walk in the ways of darkness; 14 Who rejoice to do evil, and delight in the frowardness of the wicked;

1 My son, if you will receive my words and store my commands inside you, 2 paying attention to wisdom inclining your mind toward understanding — 3 yes, if you will call for insight and raise your voice for discernment, 4 if you seek it as you would silver and search for it as for hidden treasure — 5 then you will understand the fear of the Lord and find knowledge of God. 6 For the Lord gives wisdom; from his mouth comes knowledge and understanding. 7 He stores up common sense for the upright, is a shield to those whose conduct is blameless, 8 He protects those who treat others fairly, and guards those who are devoted to him. 9 If you listen to me, you will know what is right, just, and fair. You will know what you should do. 10 You will become wise, and your knowledge will give you pleasure. 11 Your insight and understanding will protect you 12 and prevent you from doing the wrong thing. They will keep you away from people who stir up trouble by what they say— 13 those who have abandoned a righteous life to live in the darkness of sin, 14 those who find pleasure in doing wrong and who enjoy senseless evil,

15 Whose ways are crooked, and they froward in their paths: 16 To deliver thee from the strange woman, even from the stranger which flattereth with her words; 17 Which forsaketh the guide of her youth, and forgetteth the covenant of her God. 18 For her house inclineth unto death, and her paths unto the dead. 19 None that go unto her return again, neither take they hold of the paths of life. 20 That thou mayest walk in the way of good men, and keep the paths of the righteous. 21 For the upright shall dwell in the land, and the perfect shall remain in it. 22 But the wicked shall be cut off from the earth, and the transgressors shall be rooted out of it. (Proverbs 2:1-22)

15 whose tracks are twisted and whose paths are perverse (unreliable people who cannot be trusted). 16 You will be able to resist any immoral woman who tries to seduce you with her smooth talk, 17 who is faithless to her own husband and forgets her sacred vows. 18 If you go to her house, you are traveling the road to death. To go there is to approach the world of the dead. 19 No one who visits her ever comes back. He never returns to the road to life. 20 So you must follow the example of good people and live a righteous life. 21 Righteous people—people of integrity—will live in this land of ours. 22 But God will snatch the wicked from the land and pull sinners out of it like plants from the ground. (Proverbs 2:1-22)

Proverbs - Day 3

1 My son, forget not my law; but let thine heart keep my commandments: 2 For length of days, and long life, and peace, shall they add to thee. 3 Let not mercy and truth forsake thee: bind them about thy neck; write them upon the table of thine heart: 4 So shalt thou find favour and good understanding in the sight of God and man. 5 Trust in the Lord with all thine heart; and lean not unto thine own understanding. 6 In all thy ways acknowledge him, and he shall direct thy paths. 7 Be not wise in thine own eyes: fear the Lord, and depart from evil. 8 It shall be health to thy navel, and marrow to thy bones. 9 Honour the Lord with thy substance, and with the firstfruits of all thine increase: 10 So shall thy barns be filled with plenty, and thy presses shall burst out with new wine. 11 My son, despise not the chastening of the Lord; neither be weary of his correction: 12 For whom the Lord loveth he correcteth; even as a father the son in whom he delighteth. 13 Happy is the man that findeth wisdom, and the man that getteth understanding.

1 My son, don't forget my teaching, keep my commands in your heart; 2 My teaching will give you a long and prosperous life . 3 Never let go of mercy and truth. Tie them around your neck; write them on your heart. 4 If you do this, both God and people will be pleased with you. 5 Trust in the Lord with all your heart; Never rely on what you think you know. 6 Remember the Lord in everything you do, and he will show you the right way. 7 Never let yourself think that you are wiser than you are; simply obey the Lord and refuse to do wrong. 8 This will bring health to your body and give strength to your bones. 9 Honor the Lord with your wealth and with the firstfruits of all your income. 10 Then your granaries will be filled and your vats overflow with new wine. 11 My son, don't despise the Lord's discipline or resent his reproof; 12 for the Lord corrects those he loves like a father who delights in his son. 13 Happy the person who finds wisdom, the person who acquires understanding;

14 For the merchandise of it is better than the merchandise of silver, and the gain thereof than fine gold. 15 She is more precious than rubies: and all the things thou canst desire are not to be compared unto her. 16 Length of days is in her right hand; and in her left hand riches and honour. 17 Her ways are ways of pleasantness, and all her paths are peace. 18 She is a tree of life to them that lay hold upon her: and happy is every one that retaineth her. 19 The Lord by wisdom hath founded the earth; by understanding hath he established the heavens. 20 By his knowledge the depths are broken up, and the clouds drop down the dew. 21 My son, let not them depart from thine eyes: keep sound wisdom and discretion: 22 So shall they be life unto thy soul, and grace to thy neck. 23 Then shalt thou walk in thy way safely, and thy foot shall not stumble. 24 When thou liest down, thou shalt not be afraid: yea, thou shalt lie down, and thy sleep shall be sweet. 25 Be not afraid of sudden fear, neither of the desolation of the wicked, when it cometh. 26 For the Lord shall be thy confidence, and shall keep thy foot from being taken. 27 Withhold not good from them to whom it is due, when it is in the power of thine hand to do it.

14 for her profit exceeds that of silver, gaining her is better than gold, 15 she is more precious than pearls — nothing you want can compare with her. 16 Long life is in her right hand, riches and honor in her left. 17 Her ways are pleasant ways, and all her paths are peace. 18 She is a tree of life to those who grasp her; whoever holds fast to her will be made happy 19 The Lord by wisdom founded the earth, by understanding he established the heavens, 20 by his knowledge the deep [springs] burst open and the dew condenses from the sky. 21 My son, hold on to your wisdom and insight. Never let them get away from you. 22 They will provide you with life—a pleasant and happy life. 23 You can go safely on your way and never even stumble. 24 You will not be afraid when you go to bed, and you will sleep soundly through the night. 25 You will not have to worry about sudden disasters, such as come on the wicked like a storm. 26 The Lord will keep you safe. He will not let you fall into a trap. 27 Whenever you possibly can, do good to those who need it.

28 Say not unto thy neighbour, Go, and come again, and to morrow I will give; when thou hast it by thee. 29 Devise not evil against thy neighbour, seeing he dwelleth securely by thee. 30 Strive not with a man without cause, if he have done thee no harm. 31 Envy thou not the oppressor, and choose none of his ways. 32 For the froward is abomination to the Lord: but his secret is with the righteous. 33 The curse of the Lord is in the house of the wicked: but he blesseth the habitation of the just. 34 Surely he scorneth the scorners: but he giveth grace unto the lowly. 35 The wise shall inherit glory: but shame shall be the promotion of fools. (Proverbs 3:1-35)

28 Never tell your neighbors to wait until tomorrow if you can help them now. 29 Don't plan anything that will hurt your neighbors; they live beside you, trusting you. 30 Don't argue with others for no reason when they have never done you any harm. 31 Don't be jealous of violent people or decide to act as they do, 32 because the Lord hates people who do evil, but he takes righteous people into his confidence. 33 The Lord puts a curse on the homes of the wicked, but blesses the homes of the righteous. 34 He has no use for conceited people, but shows favor to those who are humble. 35 Wise people will gain an honorable reputation, but foolish people will only add to their own disgrace.

(Proverbs 3:1-35)

Proverbs - Day 4

1 Hear, ye children, the instruction of a father, and attend to know understanding. 2 For I give you good doctrine, forsake ye not my law. 3 For I was my father's son, tender and only beloved in the sight of my mother. 4 He taught me also, and said unto me, Let thine heart retain my words: keep my commandments, and live. 5 Get wisdom, get understanding: forget it not; neither decline from the words of my mouth. 6 Forsake her not, and she shall preserve thee: love her, and she shall keep thee. 7 Wisdom is the principal thing; therefore get wisdom: and with all thy getting get understanding. 8 Exalt her, and she shall promote thee: she shall bring thee to honour, when thou dost embrace her. 9 She shall give to thine head an ornament of grace: a crown of glory shall she deliver to thee. 10 Hear, O my son, and receive my sayings; and the years of thy life shall be many. 11 I have taught thee in the way of wisdom; I have led thee in right paths. 12 When thou goest, thy steps shall not be straitened; and when thou runnest, thou shalt not stumble. 13 Take fast hold of instruction; let her not go: keep her; for she is thy life.

1 Listen, children, to a father's instruction; pay attention, in order to gain insight; 2 What I am teaching you is good, so remember it all. 3 When I was only a little boy, my parents' only son, 4 my father would teach me. He would say, "Remember what I say and never forget it. Do as I tell you, and you will live. 5 Get wisdom and insight! Do not forget or ignore what I say. 6 Do not abandon wisdom, and she will protect you; love her, and she will keep you safe. 7 Getting wisdom is the most important thing you can do. Whatever else you get, get insight. 8 Love wisdom, and she will make you great. Embrace her, and she will bring you honor. 9 She will be your crowning glory." 10 Listen, my son, Take seriously what I am telling you, and you will live a long life. 11 I have taught you wisdom and the right way to live. 12 Nothing will stand in your way if you walk wisely, and you will not stumble when you run. 13 Always remember what you have learned; guard it, for it is your life.

14 Enter not into the path of the wicked, and go not in the way of evil men. 15 Avoid it, pass not by it, turn from it, and pass away. 16 For they sleep not, except they have done mischief; and their sleep is taken away, unless they cause some to fall. 17 For they eat the bread of wickedness, and drink the wine of violence. 18 But the path of the just is as the shining light, that shineth more and more unto the perfect day. 19 The way of the wicked is as darkness: they know not at what they stumble. 20 My son, attend to my words; incline thine ear unto my sayings. 21 Let them not depart from thine eyes; keep them in the midst of thine heart. 22 For they are life unto those that find them, and health to all their flesh. 23 Keep thy heart with all diligence; for out of it are the issues of life. 24 Put away from thee a froward mouth, and perverse lips put far from thee. 25 Let thine eyes look right on, and let thine eyelids look straight before thee. 26 Ponder the path of thy feet, and let all thy ways be established. 27 Turn not to the right hand nor to the left: remove thy foot from evil. (Proverbs 4:1-27)

14 Do not go where evil people go. Do not follow the example of the wicked. 15 Don't do it! Keep away from evil! Refuse it and go on your way. 16 Wicked people cannot sleep unless they have done something wrong. They lie awake unless they have hurt someone. 17 Wickedness and violence are like food and drink to them. 18 The road the righteous travel is like the sunrise, getting brighter and brighter until daylight has come. 19 The road of the wicked, however, is dark as night. They fall, but cannot see what they have stumbled over. 20 My son, pay attention to what I am saying; incline your ear to my words. 21 Never let them get away from you. Remember them and keep them in your heart. 22 They will give life and health to anyone who understands them. 23 Be careful how you think; your life is shaped by your thoughts. 24 Never say anything that isn't true. Have nothing to do with lies and misleading words. 25 Let your eyes look straight ahead, fix your gaze on what lies in front of you. 26 Plan carefully what you do, and whatever you do will turn out right. 27 Avoid evil and walk straight ahead. Don't go one step off the right way. (Proverbs 4:1-27)

Proverbs - Day 5

1 My son, attend unto my wisdom, and bow thine ear to my understanding: 2 That thou mayest regard discretion, and that thy lips may keep knowledge. 3 For the lips of a strange woman drop as an honeycomb, and her mouth is smoother than oil: 4 But her end is bitter as wormwood, sharp as a two-edged sword. 5 Her feet go down to death; her steps take hold on hell. 6 Lest thou shouldest ponder the path of life, her ways are moveable, that thou canst not know them. 7 Hear me now therefore, O ye children, and depart not from the words of my mouth. 8 Remove thy way far from her, and come not nigh the door of her house: 9 Lest thou give thine honour unto others, and thy years unto the cruel: 10 Lest strangers be filled with thy wealth; and thy labours be in the house of a stranger; 11 And thou mourn at the last, when thy flesh and thy body are consumed, 12 And say, How have I hated instruction, and my heart despised reproof; 13 And have not obeyed the voice of my teachers, nor inclined mine ear to them that instructed me! 14 I was almost in all evil in the midst of the congregation and assembly.

1 My son, pay attention and listen to my wisdom and insight. 2 Then you will know how to behave properly, and your words will show that you have knowledge. 3 The lips of another man's wife may be as sweet as honey and her kisses as smooth as olive oil, 4 but when it is all over, she leaves you nothing but bitterness and pain. 5 She will take you down to the world of the dead; the road she walks is the road to death. 6 She does not stay on the road to life; but wanders off, and does not realize what is happening. 7 Now listen to me, sons, and never forget what I am saying. 8 Keep away from such a woman! Don't even go near her door! 9 so that you won't give your vigor to others and your years to someone who is cruel, 10 so strangers won't be filled with your strength and what you worked for go to a foreign house. 11 Then, when your flesh and bones have shrunk, at the end of your life, you would moan, 12 and you will say, "Why would I never learn? Why would I never let anyone correct me? 13 I wouldn't listen to my teachers. I paid no attention to them. 14 I took part in almost every kind of evil, and the whole community knew it."

15 Drink waters out of thine own cistern, and running waters out of thine own well. 16 Let thy fountains be dispersed abroad, and rivers of waters in the streets. 17 Let them be only thine own, and not strangers' with thee. 18 Let thy fountain be blessed: and rejoice with the wife of thy youth. 19 Let her be as the loving hind and pleasant roe; let her breasts satisfy thee at all times; and be thou ravished always with her love. 20 And why wilt thou, my son, be ravished with a strange woman, and embrace the bosom of a stranger? 21 For the ways of man are before the eyes of the Lord, and he pondereth all his goings. 22 His own iniquities shall take the wicked himself, and he shall be holden with the cords of his sins. 23 He shall die without instruction; and in the greatness of his folly he shall go astray. (Proverbs 5:1-23)

15 Be faithful to your own wife and give your love to her alone. 16 Children that you have by other women will do you no good. 17 Your children should grow up to help you, not strangers. 18 So be happy with your wife and find your joy with the woman you married— 19 pretty and graceful as a deer. Let her charms keep you happy; let her surround you with her love. 20 Son, why should you give your love to another woman? Why should you prefer the charms of another man's wife? 21 The Lord sees everything you do. Wherever you go, he is watching. 22 The sins of the wicked are a trap. They get caught in the net of their own sin. 23 They die because they have no self-control. Their utter stupidity will send them to their graves. (Proverbs 5:1-23)

Proverbs - Day 6

1 My son, if thou be surety for thy friend, if thou hast stricken thy hand with a stranger, 2 Thou art snared with the words of thy mouth, thou art taken with the words of thy mouth. 3 Do this now, my son, and deliver thyself, when thou art come into the hand of thy friend; go, humble thyself, and make sure thy friend. 4 Give not sleep to thine eyes, nor slumber to thine eyelids. 5 Deliver thyself as a roe from the hand of the hunter, and as a bird from the hand of the fowler. 6 Go to the ant, thou sluggard; consider her ways, and be wise: 7 Which having no guide, overseer, or ruler, 8 Provideth her meat in the summer, and gathereth her food in the harvest. 9 How long wilt thou sleep, O sluggard? when wilt thou arise out of thy sleep? 10 Yet a little sleep, a little slumber, a little folding of the hands to sleep: 11 So shall thy poverty come as one that travelleth, and thy want as an armed man. 12 A naughty person, a wicked man, walketh with a froward mouth. 13 He winketh with his eyes, he speaketh with his feet, he teacheth with his fingers;

1 My son, have you promised to be responsible for someone else's debts? 2 Have you been caught by your own words, trapped by your own promises? 3 Well then, my son, you are in that person's power, but this is how to get out of it: hurry to him, and beg him to release you. 4 Don't let yourself go to sleep or even stop to rest. 5 Get out of the trap like a bird or a deer escaping from a hunter. 6 Lazy people should learn a lesson from the way ants live. 7 They have no leader, chief, or ruler, 8 but they store up their food during the summer, getting ready for winter. 9 How long is the lazy man going to lie around? When is he ever going to get up? 10 "I'll just take a short nap," he says; "I'll fold my hands and rest a while." 11 But while he sleeps, poverty will attack him like an armed robber. 12 Worthless, wicked people go around telling lies. 13 They wink and make gestures to deceive you,

14 Frowardness is in his heart, he deviseth mischief continually; he soweth discord. 15 Therefore shall his calamity come suddenly; suddenly shall he be broken without remedy. 16 These six things doth the Lord hate: yea, seven are an abomination unto him: 17 A proud look, a lying tongue, and hands that shed innocent blood, 18 An heart that deviseth wicked imaginations, feet that be swift in running to mischief, 19 A false witness that speaketh lies, and he that soweth discord among brethren. 20 My son, keep thy father's commandment, and forsake not the law of thy mother: 21 Bind them continually upon thine heart, and tie them about thy neck. 22 When thou goest, it shall lead thee; when thou sleepest, it shall keep thee; and when thou awakest, it shall talk with thee. 23 For the commandment is a lamp; and the law is light; and reproofs of instruction are the way of life: 24 To keep thee from the evil woman, from the flattery of the tongue of a strange woman. 25 Lust not after her beauty in thine heart; neither let her take thee with her eyelids.

14 all the while planning evil in their perverted minds, stirring up trouble everywhere. 15 Therefore disaster suddenly overcomes him; unexpectedly, he is broken beyond repair. 16 There are seven things that the Lord hates and cannot tolerate: 17 a haughty look, a lying tongue, hands that kill innocent people, 18 a mind that thinks up wicked plans, feet that hurry off to do evil, 19 a witness who tells one lie after another, and someone who stirs up trouble among friends 20 Son, do what your father tells you and never forget what your mother taught you. 21 Keep their words with you always, locked in your heart. 22 Their teaching will lead you when you travel, protect you at night, and advise you during the day. 23 Their instructions are a shining light; their correction can teach you how to live. 24 It can keep you away from bad women, from the seductive words of other men's wives. 25 Don't be tempted by their beauty; don't be trapped by their flirting eyes.

26 For by means of a whorish woman a man is brought to a piece of bread: and the adultress will hunt for the precious life. 27 Can a man take fire in his bosom, and his clothes not be burned? 28 Can one go upon hot coals, and his feet not be burned? 29 So he that goeth in to his neighbour's wife; whosoever toucheth her shall not be innocent. 30 Men do not despise a thief, if he steal to satisfy his soul when he is hungry; 31 But if he be found, he shall restore sevenfold; he shall give all the substance of his house. 32 But whoso committeth adultery with a woman lacketh understanding: he that doeth it destroyeth his own soul. 33 A wound and dishonour shall he get; and his reproach shall not be wiped away. 34 For jealousy is the rage of a man: therefore he will not spare in the day of vengeance. 35 He will not regard any ransom; neither will he rest content, though thou givest many gifts. (Proverbs 6:1-35)

26 A man can hire a prostitute for the price of a loaf of bread, but the adulteress is hunting for a precious life. 27 Can you carry fire against your chest without burning your clothes? 28 Can you walk on hot coals without burning your feet? 29 It is just as dangerous to sleep with another man's wife. Whoever does it will suffer. 30 People don't despise a thief if he steals food when he is hungry; 31 yet if he is caught, he must pay back seven times more—he must give up everything he has. 32 But a man who commits adultery doesn't have any sense. He is just destroying himself. 33 He will get nothing but blows and contempt, and his disgrace will not be wiped away. 34 A husband is never angrier than when he is jealous; his revenge knows no limits. 35 He will not accept any payment; no amount of gifts will satisfy his anger. (Proverbs 6:1-35)

Proverbs - Day 7

1 My son, keep my words, and lay up my commandments with thee. 2 Keep my commandments, and live; and my law as the apple of thine eye. 3 Bind them upon thy fingers, write them upon the table of thine heart. 4 Say unto wisdom, Thou art my sister; and call understanding thy kinswoman: 5 That they may keep thee from the strange woman, from the stranger which flattereth with her words. 6 For at the window of my house I looked through my casement, 7 And beheld among the simple ones, I discerned among the youths, a young man void of understanding, 8 Passing through the street near her corner; and he went the way to her house, 9 In the twilight, in the evening, in the black and dark night: 10 And, behold, there met him a woman with the attire of an harlot, and subtil of heart. 11 (She is loud and stubborn; her feet abide not in her house: 12 Now is she without, now in the streets, and lieth in wait at every corner.) 13 So she caught him, and kissed him, and with an impudent face said unto him,

1 My son, remember what I say and never forget what I tell you to do. 2 Do what I say, and you will live. Be as careful to follow my teaching as you are to protect your eyes. 3 Keep my teaching with you all the time; write it on your heart. 4 Treat wisdom as your sister, and insight as your closest friend. 5 They will keep you away from other men's wives, from women with seductive words. 6 Once I was looking out the window of my house, 7 and I saw many inexperienced young men, but noticed one foolish fellow in particular. 8 He was walking along the street near the corner where a certain woman lived. He was passing near her house 9 in the evening after it was dark. 10 And then she met him; she was dressed like a prostitute and was making plans. 11 She was a bold and shameless woman who always walked the streets 12 or stood waiting at a corner, sometimes in the streets, sometimes in the marketplace. 13 She threw her arms around the young man, kissed him, looked him straight in the eye, and said,

14 I have peace offerings with me; this day have I payed my vows. 15 Therefore came I forth to meet thee, diligently to seek thy face, and I have found thee. 16 I have decked my bed with coverings of tapestry, with carved works, with fine linen of Egypt. 17 I have perfumed my bed with myrrh, aloes, and cinnamon. 18 Come, let us take our fill of love until the morning: let us solace ourselves with loves. 19 For the goodman is not at home, he is gone a long journey: 20 He hath taken a bag of money with him, and will come home at the day appointed. 21 With her much fair speech she caused him to yield, with the flattering of her lips she forced him. 22 He goeth after her straightway, as an ox goeth to the slaughter, or as a fool to the correction of the stocks; 23 Till a dart strike through his liver; as a bird hasteth to the snare, and knoweth not that it is for his life. 24 Hearken unto me now therefore, O ye children, and attend to the words of my mouth. 25 Let not thine heart decline to her ways, go not astray in her paths. 26 For she hath cast down many wounded: yea, many strong men have been slain by her. 27 Her house is the way to hell, going down to the chambers of death.

(Proverbs 7:1-27)

14 "I made my offerings today and have the meat from the sacrifices. 15 So I came out looking for you. I wanted to find you, and here you are! 16 I've covered my bed with sheets of colored linen from Egypt. 17 I've perfumed it with myrrh, aloes, and cinnamon. 18 Come on! Let's make love all night long. We'll be happy in each other's arms. 19 My husband isn't at home. He's on a long trip. 20 He took plenty of money with him and won't be back for two weeks." 21 So she tempted him with her charms, and he gave in to her smooth talk. 22 At once he follows her like an ox on its way to be slaughtered; like a fool to be punished in the stocks; 23 or like a bird rushing into a trap, not knowing its life is in danger till an arrow pierces its liver. 24 Now then, children, listen to me. Pay attention to what I say. 25 Do not let such a woman win your heart; don't go wandering after her. 26 She has been the ruin of many men and caused the death of too many to count. 27 If you go to her house, you are on the way to the world of the dead. It is a shortcut to death.

(Proverbs 7:1-27)

Proverbs - Day 8

1 Doth not wisdom cry? and understanding put forth her voice? 2 She standeth in the top of high places, by the way in the places of the paths. 3 She crieth at the gates, at the entry of the city, at the coming in at the doors. 4 Unto you, O men, I call; and my voice is to the sons of man. 5 O ye simple, understand wisdom: and, ye fools, be ye of an understanding heart. 6 Hear; for I will speak of excellent things; and the opening of my lips shall be right things. 7 For my mouth shall speak truth; and wickedness is an abomination to my lips. 8 All the words of my mouth are in righteousness; there is nothing froward or perverse in them. 9 They are all plain to him that understandeth, and right to them that find knowledge. 10 Receive my instruction, and not silver; and knowledge rather than choice gold. 11 For wisdom is better than rubies; and all the things that may be desired are not to be compared to it. 12 I wisdom dwell with prudence, and find out knowledge of witty inventions. 13 The fear of the Lord is to hate evil: pride, and arrogancy, and the evil way, and the froward mouth, do I hate.

1 Listen! Wisdom is calling out. Understanding is raising her voice! 2 On the hilltops near the road and at the crossroads she stands. 3 At the entrance to the city, beside the gates, she calls: 4 "I appeal to all of you; I call to everyone on earth. 5 Are you immature? Learn to be mature. Are you foolish? Learn to have sense. 6 Listen to my excellent words; all I tell you is right. 7 What I say is the truth; lies are hateful to me. 8 Everything I say is true; nothing is false or misleading. 9 To those with insight, it is all clear; to the well-informed, it is all plain. 10 Choose my instruction instead of silver; choose knowledge rather than the finest gold. 11 "I am Wisdom, I am better than jewels; nothing you want can compare with me. 12 I am Wisdom, and I have insight; I have knowledge and sound judgment. 13 To honor the Lord is to hate evil; I hate pride and arrogance, evil ways and false words.

14 Counsel is mine, and sound wisdom: I am understanding; I have strength. 15 By me kings reign, and princes decree justice. 16 By me princes rule, and nobles, even all the judges of the earth. 17 I love them that love me; and those that seek me early shall find me. 18 Riches and honour are with me; yea, durable riches and righteousness. 19 My fruit is better than gold, yea, than fine gold; and my revenue than choice silver. 20 I lead in the way of righteousness, in the midst of the paths of judgment: 21 That I may cause those that love me to inherit substance; and I will fill their treasures. 22 The Lord possessed me in the beginning of his way, before his works of old. 23 I was set up from everlasting, from the beginning, or ever the earth was. 24 When there were no depths, I was brought forth; when there were no fountains abounding with water. 25 Before the mountains were settled, before the hills was I brought forth: 26 While as yet he had not made the earth, nor the fields, nor the highest part of the dust of the world. 27 When he prepared the heavens, I was there: when he set a compass upon the face of the depth: 28 When he established the clouds above: when he strengthened the fountains of the deep:

14 I make plans and carry them out. I have understanding, and I am strong. 15 I help kings to govern and rulers to make good laws. 16 Every ruler on earth governs with my help, officials and nobles alike. 17 I love those who love me; whoever looks for me can find me. 18 I have riches and honor to give, prosperity and success. 19 What you get from me is better than the finest gold, better than the purest silver. 20 I walk the way of righteousness; I follow the paths of justice, 21 giving wealth to those who love me, filling their houses with treasures. 22 "The Lord made me as the beginning of his way, the first of his ancient works. 23 I was appointed before the world, before the start, before the earth's beginnings. 24 When I was brought forth, there were no ocean depths, no springs brimming with water. 25 I was brought forth before the hills, before the mountains had settled in place; 26 he had not yet made the earth, the fields, or even the earth's first grains of dust. 27 I was there when he set the sky in place, when he stretched the horizon across the ocean, 28 when he placed the clouds in the sky, when he opened the springs of the ocean

29 When he gave to the sea his decree, that the waters should not pass his commandment: when he appointed the foundations of the earth: 30 Then I was by him, as one brought up with him: and I was daily his delight, rejoicing always before him; 31 Rejoicing in the habitable part of his earth; and my delights were with the sons of men. 32 Now therefore hearken unto me, O ye children: for blessed are they that keep my ways. 33 Hear instruction, and be wise, and refuse it not. 34 Blessed is the man that heareth me, watching daily at my gates, waiting at the posts of my doors. 35 For whoso findeth me findeth life, and shall obtain favour of the Lord. 36 But he that sinneth against me wrongeth his own soul: all they that hate me love death. ([Proverbs 8:1-36](#))

29 and ordered the waters of the sea to rise no further than he said. I was there when he laid the earth's foundations. 30 I was beside him like an architect, I was his daily source of joy, always happy in his presence— 31 happy with the world and pleased with the human race. 32 "Now, young people, listen to me. Do as I say, and you will be happy. 33 Listen to what you are taught. Be wise; do not neglect it. 34 Those who listen to me will be happy—

those who stay at my door every day, waiting at the entrance to my home. 35 Those who find me find life, and the Lord will be pleased with them. 36 Those who do not find me hurt themselves; anyone who hates me loves death." ([Proverbs 8:1-36](#))

Proverbs - Day 9

1 Wisdom hath builded her house, she hath hewn out her seven pillars: 2 She hath killed her beasts; she hath mingled her wine; she hath also furnished her table. 3 She hath sent forth her maidens: she crieth upon the highest places of the city, 4 Whoso is simple, let him turn in hither: as for him that wanteth understanding, she saith to him, 5 Come, eat of my bread, and drink of the wine which I have mingled. 6 Forsake the foolish, and live; and go in the way of understanding. 7 He that reproveth a scorner getteth to himself shame: and he that rebuketh a wicked man getteth himself a blot. 8 Reprove not a scorner, lest he hate thee: rebuke a wise man, and he will love thee. 9 Give instruction to a wise man, and he will be yet wiser: teach a just man, and he will increase in learning. 10 The fear of the Lord is the beginning of wisdom: and the knowledge of the holy is understanding. 11 For by me thy days shall be multiplied, and the years of thy life shall be increased. 12 If thou be wise, thou shalt be wise for thyself: but if thou scornest, thou alone shalt bear it.

1 Wisdom has built her house and made seven columns for it. 2 She has had an animal killed for a feast, mixed spices in the wine, and set the table. 3 She has sent her servant women to call out from the highest place in town: 4 "Come in, ignorant people!" And to the foolish she says, 5 "Come, eat my food and drink the wine that I have mixed. 6 Leave the company of ignorant people, and live. Follow the way of knowledge." 7 If you correct conceited people, you will only be insulted. If you reprimand evil people, you will only get hurt. 8 Never correct conceited people; they will hate you for it. But if you correct the wise, they will respect you. 9 Anything you say to the wise will make them wiser. Whatever you tell the righteous will add to their knowledge. 10 To be wise you must first have reverence for the Lord. If you know the Holy One, you have understanding. 11 Wisdom will add years to your life. 12 You are the one who will profit if you have wisdom, and if you reject it, you are the one who will suffer.

13 A foolish woman is clamorous: she is simple, and knoweth nothing. 14 For she sitteth at the door of her house, on a seat in the high places of the city, 15 To call passengers who go right on their ways: 16 Whoso is simple, let him turn in hither: and as for him that wanteth understanding, she saith to him, 17 Stolen waters are sweet, and bread eaten in secret is pleasant. 18 But he knoweth not that the dead are there; and that her guests are in the depths of hell. (Proverbs 9:1-18)

13 Stupidity is like a loud, ignorant, shameless woman. 14 She sits at the door of her house or on a seat in the highest part of town, 15 and calls out to people passing by, who are minding their own business: 16 "Come in, ignorant people!" To the foolish she says, 17 "Stolen water is sweeter. Stolen bread tastes better." 18 Her victims do not know that the people die who go to her house, that those who have already entered are now deep in the world of the dead. (Proverbs 9:1-18)

Proverbs - Day 10

1 The proverbs of Solomon. A wise son maketh a glad father: but a foolish son is the heaviness of his mother. 2 Treasures of wickedness profit nothing: but righteousness delivereth from death. 3 The Lord will not suffer the soul of the righteous to famish: but he casteth away the substance of the wicked. 4 He becometh poor that dealeth with a slack hand: but the hand of the diligent maketh rich. 5 He that gathereth in summer is a wise son: but he that sleepeth in harvest is a son that causeth shame. 6 Blessings are upon the head of the just: but violence covereth the mouth of the wicked. 7 The memory of the just is blessed: but the name of the wicked shall rot. 8 The wise in heart will receive commandments: but a prating fool shall fall. 9 He that walketh uprightly walketh surely: but he that perverteth his ways shall be known. 10 He that winketh with the eye causeth sorrow: but a prating fool shall fall. 11 The mouth of a righteous man is a well of life: but violence covereth the mouth of the wicked. 12 Hatred stirreth up strifes: but love covereth all sins.

1 These are Solomon's proverbs: A wise son is a joy to his father, but a foolish son is a grief to his mother. 2 Wealth you get by dishonesty will do you no good, but honesty can save your life. 3 The Lord will not let good people go hungry, but he thwarts the craving of the wicked. 4 Idle hands bring poverty; diligent hands bring wealth. 5 A sensible person gathers the crops when they are ready; it is a disgrace to sleep through the time of harvest. 6 Good people will receive blessings. The words of the wicked hide a violent nature. 7 Good people will be remembered as a blessing, but the wicked will soon be forgotten. 8 Wise-hearted people take orders, but a babbling fool will have trouble 9 Honest people are safe and secure, but the dishonest will be caught.
10 He who winks his eye [instead of rebuking] causes pain, yet a babbling fool will have trouble
11 A good person's words are a fountain of life, but a wicked person's words hide a violent nature. 12 Hate stirs up trouble, but love forgives all offenses.

13 In the lips of him that hath understanding wisdom is found: but a rod is for the back of him that is void of understanding. 14 Wise men lay up knowledge: but the mouth of the foolish is near destruction. 15 The rich man's wealth is his strong city: the destruction of the poor is their poverty. 16 The labour of the righteous tendeth to life: the fruit of the wicked to sin. 17 He is in the way of life that keepeth instruction: but he that refuseth reproof erreth. 18 He that hideth hatred with lying lips, and he that uttereth a slander, is a fool. 19 In the multitude of words there wanteth not sin: but he that refraineth his lips is wise. 20 The tongue of the just is as choice silver: the heart of the wicked is little worth. 21 The lips of the righteous feed many: but fools die for want of wisdom. 22 The blessing of the Lord, it maketh rich, and he addeth no sorrow with it. 23 It is as sport to a fool to do mischief: but a man of understanding hath wisdom. 24 The fear of the wicked, it shall come upon him: but the desire of the righteous shall be granted.

13 On the lips of the intelligent is found wisdom, but a stick is in store for the back of a fool. 14 The wise get all the knowledge they can, but when fools speak, trouble is not far off. 15 The wealth of the rich is his fortified city; the ruin of the poor is their poverty. 16 The activity of the righteous is for life; the income of the wicked is for sin. 17 He who observes discipline is on the way to life; but he who ignores correction is making a mistake. 18 Anyone who hides hatred is a liar. Anyone who spreads gossip is a fool. 19 The more you talk, the more likely you are to sin. If you are wise, you will keep quiet. 20 A good person's words are like pure silver; a wicked person's ideas are worthless. 21 A good person's words will benefit many people, but you can kill yourself with stupidity. 22 the blessing of the Lord is what makes people rich, and he doesn't mix sorrow with it 23 It is foolish to enjoy doing wrong. Intelligent people take pleasure in wisdom. 24 The righteous get what they want, but the wicked will get what they fear most.

25 As the whirlwind passeth, so is the wicked no more: but the righteous is an everlasting foundation. 26 As vinegar to the teeth, and as smoke to the eyes, so is the sluggard to them that send him. 27 The fear of the Lord prolongeth days: but the years of the wicked shall be shortened. 28 The hope of the righteous shall be gladness: but the expectation of the wicked shall perish. 29 The way of the Lord is strength to the upright: but destruction shall be to the workers of iniquity. 30 The righteous shall never be removed: but the wicked shall not inhabit the earth. 31 The mouth of the just bringeth forth wisdom: but the froward tongue shall be cut out. 32 The lips of the righteous know what is acceptable: but the mouth of the wicked speaketh frowardness. (Proverbs 10:1-32)

25 When the storm has passed, the wicked are gone; but the righteous are firmly established forever. 26 Never get a lazy person to do something for you; he will be as irritating as vinegar on your teeth or smoke in your eyes. 27 Obey the Lord, and you will live longer. The wicked die before their time. 28 The hopes of good people lead to joy, but wicked people can look forward to nothing. 29 The Lord protects honest people, but destroys those who do wrong. 30 Righteous people will always have security, but the wicked will not survive in the land. 31 Righteous people speak wisdom, but the tongue that speaks evil will be stopped. 32 Righteous people know the kind thing to say, but the wicked are always saying things that hurt." (Proverbs 10:1-32)

Proverbs - Day 11

1 A false balance is abomination to the Lord: but a just weight is his delight. 2 When pride cometh, then cometh shame: but with the lowly is wisdom. 3 The integrity of the upright shall guide them: but the perverseness of transgressors shall destroy them. 4 Riches profit not in the day of wrath: but righteousness delivereth from death. 5 The righteousness of the perfect shall direct his way: but the wicked shall fall by his own wickedness. 6 The righteousness of the upright shall deliver them: but transgressors shall be taken in their own naughtiness. 7 When a wicked man dieth, his expectation shall perish: and the hope of unjust men perisheth. 8 The righteous is delivered out of trouble, and the wicked cometh in his stead. 9 An hypocrite with his mouth destroyeth his neighbour: but through knowledge shall the just be delivered. 10 When it goeth well with the righteous, the city rejoiceth: and when the wicked perish, there is shouting. 11 By the blessing of the upright the city is exalted: but it is overthrown by the mouth of the wicked. 12 He that is void of wisdom despiseth his neighbour: but a man of understanding holdeth his peace.

1 The Lord hates people who use dishonest scales. He is happy with honest weights. 2 People who are proud will soon be disgraced. It is wiser to be modest. 3 If you are good, you are guided by honesty. People who can't be trusted are destroyed by their own dishonesty. 4 Riches will do you no good on the day you face death, but honesty can save your life. 5 Honesty makes a good person's life easier, but the wicked will cause their own downfall. 6 Righteousness rescues those who are honest, but those who can't be trusted are trapped by their own greed. 7 When the wicked die, their hope dies with them. Confidence placed in riches comes to nothing. 8 The righteous are protected from trouble; it comes to the wicked instead. 9 You can be ruined by the talk of godless people, but the wisdom of the righteous can save you. 10 A city is happy when honest people have good fortune, and there are joyful shouts when the wicked die. 11 A city becomes great when the righteous give it their blessing; but a city is brought to ruin by the words of the wicked. 12 It is foolish to speak scornfully of others. If you are smart, you will keep quiet.

13 A talebearer revealeth secrets: but he that is of a faithful spirit concealeth the matter. 14 Where no counsel is, the people fall: but in the multitude of counsellors there is safety. 15 He that is surety for a stranger shall smart for it: and he that hateth suretiship is sure. 16 A gracious woman retaineth honour: and strong men retain riches. 17 The merciful man doeth good to his own soul: but he that is cruel troubleth his own flesh. 18 The wicked worketh a deceitful work: but to him that soweth righteousness shall be a sure reward. 19 As righteousness tendeth to life: so he that pursueth evil pursueth it to his own death. 20 They that are of a froward heart are abomination to the Lord: but such as are upright in their way are his delight. 21 Though hand join in hand, the wicked shall not be unpunished: but the seed of the righteous shall be delivered. 22 As a jewel of gold in a swine's snout, so is a fair woman which is without discretion. 23 The desire of the righteous is only good: but the expectation of the wicked is wrath.

13 No one who gossips can be trusted with a secret, but you can put confidence in someone who is trustworthy. 14 A nation will fall if it has no guidance. Many advisers mean security. 15 If you promise to pay a stranger's debt, you will regret it. You are better off if you don't get involved. 16 A gracious woman obtains honor; aggressive men obtain wealth. 17 You do yourself a favor when you are kind. If you are cruel, you only hurt yourself. 18 Wicked people do not really gain anything, but if you do what is right, you are certain to be rewarded. 19 Anyone who is determined to do right will live, but anyone who insists on doing wrong will die. 20 The Lord hates evil-minded people, but loves those who do right. 21 You can be sure that evil people will be punished, but the righteous will escape. 22 Beauty in a woman without good judgment is like a gold ring in a pig's snout. 23 What good people want always results in good; when the wicked get what they want, everyone is angry.

24 There is that scattereth, and yet increaseth; and there is that withholdeth more than is meet, but it tendeth to poverty. 25 The liberal soul shall be made fat: and he that watereth shall be watered also himself. 26 He that withholdeth corn, the people shall curse him: but blessing shall be upon the head of him that selleth it. 27 He that diligently seeketh good procureth favour: but he that seeketh mischief, it shall come unto him. 28 He that trusteth in his riches shall fall; but the righteous shall flourish as a branch. 29 He that troubleth his own house shall inherit the wind: and the fool shall be servant to the wise of heart. 30 The fruit of the righteous is a tree of life; and he that winneth souls is wise. 31 Behold, the righteous shall be recompensed in the earth: much more the wicked and the sinner. (Proverbs 11:1-31)

24 Some give freely and still get richer, while others are stingy but grow still poorer. 25 Be generous, and you will be prosperous. Help others, and you will be helped. 26 People curse someone who hoards grain, waiting for a higher price, but they praise the one who puts it up for sale. 27 If your goals are good, you will be respected, but if you are looking for trouble, that is what you will get. 28 Those who depend on their wealth will fall like the leaves of autumn, but the righteous will prosper like the leaves of summer. 29 Those who bring trouble on their families will have nothing at the end. Foolish people will always be servants to the wise. 30 Righteousness gives life, but violence takes it away. 31 Those who are good are rewarded here on earth, so you can be sure that wicked and sinful people will be punished. (Proverbs 11:1-31)

Proverbs - Day 12

1 Whoso loveth instruction loveth knowledge: but he that hateth reproof is brutish. 2 A good man obtaineth favour of the Lord: but a man of wicked devices will he condemn. 3 A man shall not be established by wickedness: but the root of the righteous shall not be moved. 4 A virtuous woman is a crown to her husband: but she that maketh ashamed is as rottenness in his bones. 5 The thoughts of the righteous are right: but the counsels of the wicked are deceit. 6 The words of the wicked are to lie in wait for blood: but the mouth of the upright shall deliver them. 7 The wicked are overthrown, and are not: but the house of the righteous shall stand. 8 A man shall be commended according to his wisdom: but he that is of a perverse heart shall be despised. 9 He that is despised, and hath a servant, is better than he that honoureth himself, and lacketh bread. 10 A righteous man regardeth the life of his beast: but the tender mercies of the wicked are cruel. 11 He that tilleth his land shall be satisfied with bread: but he that followeth vain persons is void of understanding. 12 The wicked desireth the net of evil men: but the root of the righteous yieldeth fruit.

1 Any who love knowledge want to be told when they are wrong. It is foolish to hate being corrected. 2 The Lord is pleased with good people, but condemns those who plan evil. 3 Wickedness does not give security, but righteous people stand firm. 4 A good wife is her husband's pride and joy; but a wife who brings shame on her husband is like a cancer in his bones. 5 Honest people will treat you fairly; the wicked only want to deceive you. 6 The words of the wicked are murderous, but the words of the righteous rescue those who are threatened. 7 The wicked meet their downfall and leave no descendants, but the families of the righteous live on. 8 A person wins praise in keeping with his common sense, but a person with a warped mind is treated with contempt. 9 It is better to be an ordinary person working for a living than to play the part of someone great but go hungry. 10 Good people take care of their animals, but wicked people are cruel to theirs. 11 A hard-working farmer has plenty to eat, but it is foolish to waste time on useless projects. 12 All that wicked people want is to find evil things to do, but the righteous stand firm.

13 The wicked is snared by the transgression of his lips: but the just shall come out of trouble. 14 A man shall be satisfied with good by the fruit of his mouth: and the recompence of a man's hands shall be rendered unto him. 15 The way of a fool is right in his own eyes: but he that hearkeneth unto counsel is wise. 16 A fool's wrath is presently known: but a prudent man covereth shame. 17 He that speaketh truth sheweth forth righteousness: but a false witness deceit. 18 There is that speaketh like the piercings of a sword: but the tongue of the wise is health. 19 The lip of truth shall be established for ever: but a lying tongue is but for a moment. 20 Deceit is in the heart of them that imagine evil: but to the counsellors of peace is joy. 21 There shall no evil happen to the just: but the wicked shall be filled with mischief. 22 Lying lips are abomination to the Lord: but they that deal truly are his delight. 23 A prudent man concealeth knowledge: but the heart of fools proclaimeth foolishness. 24 The hand of the diligent shall bear rule: but the slothful shall be under tribute. 25 Heaviness in the heart of man maketh it stoop: but a good word maketh it glad.

13 The wicked are trapped by their own words, but honest people get themselves out of trouble. 14 Your reward depends on what you say and what you do; you will get what you deserve. 15 Foolish people always think they are right. Wise people listen to advice. 16 When a fool is annoyed, he quickly lets it be known. Smart people will ignore an insult. 17 When you tell the truth, justice is done, but lies lead to injustice. 18 Thoughtless words can wound as deeply as any sword, but wisely spoken words can heal. 19 A lie has a short life, but truth lives on forever. 20 Deceit is in the hearts of those who plot evil, but for those advising peace there is joy. 21 No harm can come to the righteous, but the wicked are overwhelmed with disaster. 22 The Lord hates liars, but is pleased with those who keep their word. 23 Smart people keep quiet about what they know, but foolish people advertise their ignorance. 24 The diligent will rule, while the lazy will be put to forced labor. 25 Worry can rob you of happiness, but kind words will cheer you up.

26 The righteous is more excellent than his neighbour: but the way of the wicked seduceth them. 27 The slothful man roasteth not that which he took in hunting: but the substance of a diligent man is precious. 28 In the way of righteousness is life: and in the pathway thereof there is no death. (Proverbs 12:1-28)

26 The righteous person is a guide to his friend, but the path of the wicked leads them astray. 27 If you are lazy, you will never get what you are after, but if you work hard, you will get a fortune. 28 Righteousness is the road to life; wickedness is the road to death. (Proverbs 12:1-28)

Proverbs - Day 13

1 A wise son heareth his father's instruction: but a scorner heareth not rebuke. 2 A man shall eat good by the fruit of his mouth: but the soul of the transgressors shall eat violence. 3 He that keepeth his mouth keepeth his life: but he that openeth wide his lips shall have destruction. 4 The soul of the sluggard desireth, and hath nothing: but the soul of the diligent shall be made fat. 5 A righteous man hateth lying: but a wicked man is loathsome, and cometh to shame. 6 Righteousness keepeth him that is upright in the way: but wickedness overthroweth the sinner. 7 There is that maketh himself rich, yet hath nothing: there is that maketh himself poor, yet hath great riches. 8 The ransom of a man's life are his riches: but the poor heareth not rebuke. 9 The light of the righteous rejoiceth: but the lamp of the wicked shall be put out. 10 Only by pride cometh contention: but with the well advised is wisdom. 11 Wealth gotten by vanity shall be diminished: but he that gathereth by labour shall increase. 12 Hope deferred maketh the heart sick: but when the desire cometh, it is a tree of life.

1 A son who heeds his father's discipline is wise, but arrogant people never admit they are wrong. 2 A [good] man enjoys good as a result of what he says, but the essence of the treacherous is violence. 3 Be careful what you say and protect your life. A careless talker destroys himself. 4 No matter how much a lazy person may want something, he will never get it. A hard worker will get everything he wants. 5 Honest people hate lies, but the words of wicked people are shameful and disgraceful. 6 Righteousness protects the innocent; wickedness is the downfall of sinners. 7 Some people pretend to be rich, but have nothing. Others pretend to be poor, but own a fortune. 8 The rich man may have to ransom his life, but a poor man gets no threats. 9 The righteous are like a light shining brightly; the wicked are like a lamp flickering out. 10 Arrogance causes nothing but trouble. It is wiser to ask for advice. 11 The Wealth gotten by worthless means dwindles away, but he who amasses it by hard work will increase it. 12 When hope is crushed, the heart is crushed, but a wish come true fills you with joy.

13 Whoso despiseth the word shall be destroyed: but he that feareth the commandment shall be rewarded. 14 The law of the wise is a fountain of life, to depart from the snares of death. 15 Good understanding giveth favour: but the way of transgressors is hard. 16 Every prudent man dealeth with knowledge: but a fool layeth open his folly. 17 A wicked messenger falleth into mischief: but a faithful ambassador is health. 18 Poverty and shame shall be to him that refuseth instruction: but he that regardeth reproof shall be honoured. 19 The desire accomplished is sweet to the soul: but it is abomination to fools to depart from evil. 20 He that walketh with wise men shall be wise: but a companion of fools shall be destroyed. 21 Evil pursueth sinners: but to the righteous good shall be repayed. 22 A good man leaveth an inheritance to his children's children: and the wealth of the sinner is laid up for the just. 23 Much food is in the tillage of the poor: but there is that is destroyed for want of judgment. 24 He that spareth his rod hateth his son: but he that loveth him chasteneth him betimes. 25 The righteous eateth to the satisfying of his soul: but the belly of the wicked shall want. (Proverbs 13:1-25)

13 If you refuse good advice, you are asking for trouble; follow it and you are safe. 14 The teachings of the wise are a fountain of life; they will help you escape when your life is in danger. 15 Intelligence wins respect, but those who can't be trusted are on the road to ruin. 16 Sensible people always think before they act, but foolish people advertise their ignorance. 17 Unreliable messengers cause trouble, but those who can be trusted bring peace. 18 Someone who will not learn will be poor and disgraced. Anyone who listens to correction is respected. 19 Desire fulfilled is sweet to the soul, but turning away from evil is abhorrent to fools. 20 Keep company with the wise and you will become wise. If you make friends with foolish people, you will be ruined. 21 Trouble follows sinners everywhere, but righteous people will be rewarded with good things. 22 Good people will have wealth to leave to their grandchildren, but the wealth of sinners will go to the righteous. 23 Unused fields could yield plenty of food for the poor, but unjust people keep them from being farmed. 24 If you don't punish your children, you don't love them. If you do love them, you will correct them. 25 The righteous have enough to eat, but the wicked are always hungry. (Proverbs 13:1-25)

Proverbs - Day 14

1 Every wise woman buildeth her house: but the foolish plucketh it down with her hands. 2 He that walketh in his uprightness feareth the Lord: but he that is perverse in his ways despiseth him. 3 In the mouth of the foolish is a rod of pride: but the lips of the wise shall preserve them. 4 Where no oxen are, the crib is clean: but much increase is by the strength of the ox. 5 A faithful witness will not lie: but a false witness will utter lies. 6 A scorner seeketh wisdom, and findeth it not: but knowledge is easy unto him that understandeth. 7 Go from the presence of a foolish man, when thou perceivest not in him the lips of knowledge. 8 The wisdom of the prudent is to understand his way: but the folly of fools is deceit. 9 Fools make a mock at sin: but among the righteous there is favour. 10 The heart knoweth his own bitterness; and a stranger doth not intermeddle with his joy. 11 The house of the wicked shall be overthrown: but the tabernacle of the upright shall flourish. 12 There is a way which seemeth right unto a man, but the end thereof are the ways of death. 13 Even in laughter the heart is sorrowful; and the end of that mirth is heaviness.

1 Every wise woman builds up her home, but a foolish one tears it down with her own hands. 2 Be honest and you show that you have reverence for the Lord; be dishonest and you show that you do not. 3 Proud fools talk too much; the words of the wise protect them. 4 Without any oxen to pull the plow your barn will be empty, but with them it will be full of grain. 5 A reliable witness always tells the truth, but an unreliable one tells nothing but lies. 6 Conceited people can never become wise, but intelligent people learn easily. 7 Stay away from foolish people; they have nothing to teach you. 8 Why is a clever person wise? Because he knows what to do. Why is a stupid person foolish? Because he only thinks he knows. 9 Foolish people don't care if they sin, but among the upright there is good will. 10 Your joy is your own; your bitterness is your own. No one can share them with you. 11 A good person's house will still be standing after an evildoer's house has been destroyed. 12 What you think is the right road may lead to death. 13 Even in laughter the heart can be sad, and joy may end in sorrow.

14 The backslider in heart shall be filled with his own ways: and a good man shall be satisfied from himself. 15 The simple believeth every word: but the prudent man looketh well to his going. 16 A wise man feareth, and departeth from evil: but the fool rageth, and is confident. 17 He that is soon angry dealeth foolishly: and a man of wicked devices is hated. 18 The simple inherit folly: but the prudent are crowned with knowledge. 19 The evil bow before the good; and the wicked at the gates of the righteous. 20 The poor is hated even of his own neighbour: but the rich hath many friends. 21 He that despiseth his neighbour sinneth: but he that hath mercy on the poor, happy is he. 22 Do they not err that devise evil? but mercy and truth shall be to them that devise good. 23 In all labour there is profit: but the talk of the lips tendeth only to penury. 24 The crown of the wise is their riches: but the foolishness of fools is folly. 25 A true witness delivereth souls: but a deceitful witness speaketh lies. 26 In the fear of the Lord is strong confidence: and his children shall have a place of refuge.

14 A backslider is filled up with his own ways, but a good person gets satisfaction from himself. 15 A fool will believe anything; smart people watch their step. 16 Sensible people are careful to stay out of trouble, but foolish people are careless and act too quickly. 17 He who is quick-tempered does stupid things, and one who does vile things is hated. 18 Ignorant people get what their foolishness deserves, but the clever are rewarded with knowledge. 19 Evil people will have to bow down to the righteous and humbly beg their favor. 20 No one likes the poor, not even their neighbors, but the rich have many friends. 21 If you want to be happy, be kind to the poor; it is a sin to despise anyone. 22 Won't those who plot evil go astray? But grace and truth are for those who plan good. 23 Work and you will earn a living; but mere talk produces only poverty. 24 Wise people are rewarded with wealth, but fools are known by their foolishness. 25 A witness saves lives when he tells the truth; when he tells lies, he betrays people. 26 Reverence for the Lord gives confidence and security to a man and his family.

27 The fear of the Lord is a fountain of life, to depart from the snares of death. 28 In the multitude of people is the king's honour: but in the want of people is the destruction of the prince. 29 He that is slow to wrath is of great understanding: but he that is hasty of spirit exalteth folly. 30 A sound heart is the life of the flesh: but envy the rottenness of the bones. 31 He that oppresseth the poor reproacheth his Maker: but he that honoureth him hath mercy on the poor. 32 The wicked is driven away in his wickedness: but the righteous hath hope in his death. 33 Wisdom resteth in the heart of him that hath understanding: but that which is in the midst of fools is made known. 34 Righteousness exalteth a nation: but sin is a reproach to any people. 35 The king's favour is toward a wise servant: but his wrath is against him that causeth shame. (Proverbs 14:1-35)

27 Do you want to avoid death? Reverence for the Lord is a fountain of life. 28 A king's greatness depends on how many people he rules; without them he is nothing. 29 If you stay calm, you are wise, but if you have a hot temper, you only show how foolish you are. 30 Peace of mind makes the body healthy, but jealousy is like a cancer. 31 The oppressor of the poor insults his maker, but he who is kind to the needy honors him. 32 Wicked people bring about their own downfall by their evil deeds, but good people are protected by their integrity. 33 Wisdom is in every thought of intelligent people; fools know nothing about wisdom. 34 Righteousness makes a nation great; sin is a disgrace to any nation. 35 Kings are pleased with competent officials, but they punish those who fail them. (Proverbs 14:1-35)

Proverbs - Day 15

1 A soft answer turneth away wrath: but grievous words stir up anger. 2 The tongue of the wise useth knowledge aright: but the mouth of fools poureth out foolishness. 3 The eyes of the Lord are in every place, beholding the evil and the good. 4 A wholesome tongue is a tree of life: but perverseness therein is a breach in the spirit. 5 A fool despiseth his father's instruction: but he that regardeth reproof is prudent. 6 In the house of the righteous is much treasure: but in the revenues of the wicked is trouble. 7 The lips of the wise disperse knowledge: but the heart of the foolish doeth not so. 8 The sacrifice of the wicked is an abomination to the Lord: but the prayer of the upright is his delight. 9 The way of the wicked is an abomination unto the Lord: but he loveth him that followeth after righteousness. 10 Correction is grievous unto him that forsaketh the way: and he that hateth reproof shall die. 11 Hell and destruction are before the Lord: how much more then the hearts of the children of men? 12 A scorner loveth not one that reproveth him: neither will he go unto the wise.

1 A gentle answer quiets anger, but a harsh one stirs it up. 2 When wise people speak, they make knowledge attractive, but foolish people spout nonsense. 3 The Lord sees what happens everywhere; he is watching us, whether we do good or evil. 4 Kind words bring life, but cruel words crush your spirit. 5 It is foolish to ignore what your parents taught you; it is wise to accept their correction. 6 Righteous people keep their wealth, but the wicked lose theirs when hard times come. 7 Knowledge is spread by people who are wise, not by fools. 8 The Lord detests the sacrifices of the wicked but delights in the prayers of the upright. 9 The Lord hates the ways of evil people, but loves those who do what is right. 10 If you do what is wrong, you will be severely punished; you will die if you do not let yourself be corrected. 11 Not even the world of the dead can keep the Lord from knowing what is there; how then can we hide our thoughts from God? 12 Conceited people do not like to be corrected; they never ask for advice from those who are wiser.

13 A merry heart maketh a cheerful countenance: but by sorrow of the heart the spirit is broken. 14 The heart of him that hath understanding seeketh knowledge: but the mouth of fools feedeth on foolishness. 15 All the days of the afflicted are evil: but he that is of a merry heart hath a continual feast. 16 Better is little with the fear of the Lord than great treasure and trouble therewith. 17 Better is a dinner of herbs where love is, than a stalled ox and hatred therewith. 18 A wrathful man stirreth up strife: but he that is slow to anger appeaseth strife. 19 The way of the slothful man is as an hedge of thorns: but the way of the righteous is made plain. 20 A wise son maketh a glad father: but a foolish man despiseth his mother. 21 Folly is joy to him that is destitute of wisdom: but a man of understanding walketh uprightly. 22 Without counsel purposes are disappointed: but in the multitude of counsellors they are established. 23 A man hath joy by the answer of his mouth: and a word spoken in due season, how good is it! 24 The way of life is above to the wise, that he may depart from hell beneath. 25 The Lord will destroy the house of the proud: but he will establish the border of the widow.

13 When people are happy, they smile, but heartache breaks the spirit. 14 Intelligent people want to learn, but foolish people are satisfied with ignorance. 15 The life of the poor is a constant struggle, but happy people always enjoy life. 16 Better to be poor and fear the Lord than to be rich and in trouble. 17 Better to eat vegetables with people you love than to eat the finest meat where there is hate. 18 Hot tempers cause arguments, but patience brings peace. 19 If you are lazy, you will meet difficulty everywhere, but if you are honest, you will have no trouble. 20 A wise son is a joy to his father, and only a fool despises his mother . 21 Stupid people are happy with their foolishness, but the wise will do what is right. 22 Without deliberation, plans go wrong; but with many advisers, they succeed. 23 What a joy it is to find just the right word for the right occasion! 24 Wise people walk the road that leads upward to life, not the road that leads downward to death. 25 The Lord will destroy the homes of arrogant men, but he will protect a widow's property.

26 The thoughts of the wicked are an abomination to the Lord: but the words of the pure are pleasant words. 27 He that is greedy of gain troubleth his own house; but he that hateth gifts shall live. 28 The heart of the righteous studieth to answer: but the mouth of the wicked poureth out evil things. 29 The Lord is far from the wicked: but he heareth the prayer of the righteous. 30 The light of the eyes rejoiceth the heart: and a good report maketh the bones fat. 31 The ear that heareth the reproof of life abideth among the wise. 32 He that refuseth instruction despiseth his own soul: but he that heareth reproof getteth understanding. 33 The fear of the Lord is the instruction of wisdom; and before honour is humility. (Proverbs 15:1-33)

26 The Lord hates evil thoughts, but he is pleased with friendly words. 27 Try to make a profit dishonestly, and you get your family in trouble. Don't take bribes and you will live longer. 28 Good people think before they answer. Evil people have a quick reply, but it causes trouble. 29 When good people pray, the Lord listens, but he ignores those who are evil. 30 Smiling faces make you happy, and good news makes you feel better. 31 If you pay attention when you are corrected, you are wise. 32 If you refuse to learn, you are hurting yourself. If you accept correction, you will become wiser. 33 Reverence for the Lord is an education in itself. You must be humble before you can ever receive honors. (Proverbs 15:1-33)

Proverbs - Day 16

1 The preparations of the heart in man, and the answer of the tongue, is from the Lord. 2 All the ways of a man are clean in his own eyes; but the Lord weigheth the spirits. 3 Commit thy works unto the Lord, and thy thoughts shall be established. 4 The Lord hath made all things for himself: yea, even the wicked for the day of evil. 5 Every one that is proud in heart is an abomination to the Lord: though hand join in hand, he shall not be unpunished. 6 By mercy and truth iniquity is purged: and by the fear of the Lord men depart from evil. 7 When a man's ways please the Lord, he maketh even his enemies to be at peace with him. 8 Better is a little with righteousness than great revenues without right. 9 A man's heart deviseth his way: but the Lord directeth his steps. 10 A divine sentence is in the lips of the king: his mouth transgresseth not in judgment. 11 A just weight and balance are the Lord's: all the weights of the bag are his work. 12 It is an abomination to kings to commit wickedness: for the throne is established by righteousness. 13 Righteous lips are the delight of kings; and they love him that speaketh right.

1 A person is responsible to prepare his heart, but how the tongue speaks is from the Lord. 2 You may think everything you do is right, but the Lord judges your motives. 3 If you entrust all you do to the Lord, your plans will achieve success. 4 The Lord made everything for its purpose, even the wicked for the day of disaster . 5 The Lord hates everyone who is arrogant; he will never let them escape punishment. 6 Grace and truth atone for iniquity, and people turn from evil through fear of the Lord . 7 When you please the Lord, you can make your enemies into friends. 8 It is better to have a little, honestly earned, than to have a large income, dishonestly gained. 9 You may make your plans, but God directs your actions. 10 The king speaks with divine authority; so his mouth must be faithful when he judges. 11 The Lord wants weights and measures to be honest and every sale to be fair. 12 It is an abomination for a king to do evil, for the throne is made secure by righteousness. 13 The king should delight in righteous lips, and he should love someone who speaks what is right.

14 The wrath of a king is as messengers of death: but a wise man will pacify it. 15 In the light of the king's countenance is life; and his favour is as a cloud of the latter rain. 16 How much better is it to get wisdom than gold! and to get understanding rather to be chosen than silver! 17 The highway of the upright is to depart from evil: he that keepeth his way preserveth his soul. 18 Pride goeth before destruction, and an haughty spirit before a fall. 19 Better it is to be of an humble spirit with the lowly, than to divide the spoil with the proud. 20 He that handleth a matter wisely shall find good: and whoso trusteth in the Lord, happy is he. 21 The wise in heart shall be called prudent: and the sweetness of the lips increaseth learning. 22 Understanding is a wellspring of life unto him that hath it: but the instruction of fools is folly. 23 The heart of the wise teacheth his mouth, and addeth learning to his lips. 24 Pleasant words are as an honeycomb, sweet to the soul, and health to the bones. 25 There is a way that seemeth right unto a man, but the end thereof are the ways of death. 26 He that laboureth laboureth for himself; for his mouth craveth it of him. 27 An ungodly man diggeth up evil: and in his lips there is as a burning fire.

14 The king's anger is a herald of death, and one who is wise will appease it. 15 When the king's face brightens, it means life; his favor is like the clouds that bring spring rain. 16 It is better—much better—to have wisdom and knowledge than gold and silver. 17 Those who are good travel a road that avoids evil; so watch where you are going—it may save your life. 18 Pride leads to destruction, and arrogance to downfall. 19 It is better to be humble and stay poor than to be one of the arrogant and get a share of their loot. 20 He who has skill in a matter will succeed; he who trusts in Adonai will be happy. 21 A wise, mature person is known for his understanding. The more pleasant his words, the more persuasive he is. 22 Wisdom is a fountain of life to the wise, but trying to educate foolish people is a waste of time. 23 Intelligent people think before they speak; what they say is then more persuasive. 24 Kind words are like honey—sweet to the taste and good for your health. 25 What you think is the right road may lead to death. 26 A laborer's appetite makes him work harder, because he wants to satisfy his hunger. 27 Evil people look for ways to harm others; even their words burn with evil.

28 A froward man soweth strife: and a whisperer separateth chief friends. 29 A violent man enticeth his neighbour, and leadeth him into the way that is not good. 30 He shutteth his eyes to devise froward things: moving his lips he bringeth evil to pass. 31 The hoary head is a crown of glory, if it be found in the way of righteousness. 32 He that is slow to anger is better than the mighty; and he that ruleth his spirit than he that taketh a city. 33 The lot is cast into the lap; but the whole disposing thereof is of the Lord. ([Proverbs 16:1-33](#))

28 Gossip is spread by wicked people; they stir up trouble and break up friendships. 29 Violent people deceive their friends and lead them to disaster. 30 Watch out for people who grin and wink at you; they have thought of something evil. 31 Long life is the reward of the righteous; gray hair is a glorious crown. 32 It is better to be patient than powerful. It is better to win control over yourself than over whole cities. 33 People cast lots to learn God's will, but God himself determines the answer. ([Proverbs 16:1-33](#))

Proverbs - Day 17

1 Better is a dry morsel, and quietness therewith, than an house full of sacrifices with strife. 2 A wise servant shall have rule over a son that causeth shame, and shall have part of the inheritance among the brethren. 3 The fining pot is for silver, and the furnace for gold: but the Lord trieth the hearts. 4 A wicked doer giveth heed to false lips; and a liar giveth ear to a naughty tongue. 5 Whoso mocketh the poor reproacheth his Maker: and he that is glad at calamities shall not be unpunished. 6 Children's children are the crown of old men; and the glory of children are their fathers. 7 Excellent speech becometh not a fool: much less do lying lips a prince. 8 A gift is as a precious stone in the eyes of him that hath it: whithersoever it turneth, it prospereth. 9 He that covereth a transgression seeketh love; but he that repeateth a matter separateth very friends. 10 A reproof entereth more into a wise man than an hundred stripes into a fool. 11 An evil man seeketh only rebellion: therefore a cruel messenger shall be sent against him.

1 Better to eat a dry crust of bread with peace of mind than have a banquet in a house full of trouble. 2 A shrewd servant will gain authority over a master's worthless son and receive a part of the inheritance. 3 Gold and silver are tested by fire, and a person's heart is tested by the Lord. 4 Evil people listen to evil ideas, and liars listen to lies. 5 If you make fun of poor people, you insult the God who made them. You will be punished if you take pleasure in someone's misfortune. 6 Grandparents are proud of their grandchildren, just as children are proud of their parents. 7 Fine speech is unbecoming to a fool, and even less lying lips to a leader. 8 A bribe works like a charm, in the view of him who gives it — wherever it turns, it succeeds. 9 He who conceals an offense promotes love, but he who harps on it can separate even close friends. 10 An intelligent person learns more from one rebuke than a fool learns from being beaten a hundred times. 11 An evil person seeks only rebellion, but a cruel messenger will be sent against him.

12 Let a bear robbed of her whelps meet a man, rather than a fool in his folly. 13 Whoso rewardeth evil for good, evil shall not depart from his house. 14 The beginning of strife is as when one letteth out water: therefore leave off contention, before it be meddled with. 15 He that justifieth the wicked, and he that condemneth the just, even they both are abomination to the Lord. 16 Wherefore is there a price in the hand of a fool to get wisdom, seeing he hath no heart to it? 17 A friend loveth at all times, and a brother is born for adversity. 18 A man void of understanding striketh hands, and becometh surety in the presence of his friend. 19 He loveth transgression that loveth strife: and he that exalteth his gate seeketh destruction. 20 He that hath a froward heart findeth no good: and he that hath a perverse tongue falleth into mischief. 21 He that begetteth a fool doeth it to his sorrow: and the father of a fool hath no joy. 22 A merry heart doeth good like a medicine: but a broken spirit drieth the bones. 23 A wicked man taketh a gift out of the bosom to pervert the ways of judgment. 24 Wisdom is before him that hath understanding; but the eyes of a fool are in the ends of the earth.

12 It is better to meet a mother bear robbed of her cubs than to meet some fool busy with a stupid project. 13 If you repay good with evil, you will never get evil out of your house. 14 The start of an argument is like the first break in a dam; stop it before it goes any further. 15 Condemning the innocent or letting the wicked go—both are hateful to the Lord. 16 Why would a fool wish to pay for wisdom when he has no desire to learn? 17 Friends always show their love. What are relatives for if not to share trouble? 18 Only someone with no sense would promise to be responsible for someone else's debts. 19 To like sin is to like making trouble. If you brag all the time, you are asking for trouble. 20 Anyone who thinks and speaks evil can expect to find nothing good—only disaster. 21 There is nothing but sadness and sorrow for parents whose children do foolish things. 22 Being cheerful keeps you healthy. It is slow death to be gloomy all the time. 23 From under a cloak a bad man takes a bribe to pervert the course of justice . 24 An intelligent person aims at wise action, but a fool starts off in many directions.

25 A foolish son is a grief to his father, and bitterness to her that bare him. 26 Also to punish the just is not good, nor to strike princes for equity. 27 He that hath knowledge spareth his words: and a man of understanding is of an excellent spirit. 28 Even a fool, when he holdeth his peace, is counted wise: and he that shutteth his lips is esteemed a man of understanding. (Proverbs 17:1-28)

25 Foolish children bring grief to their fathers and bitter regrets to their mothers. 26 It is not right to make an innocent person pay a fine; justice is perverted when good people are punished. 27 Those who are sure of themselves do not talk all the time. People who stay calm have real insight. 28 After all, even fools may be thought wise and intelligent if they stay quiet and keep their mouths shut. (Proverbs 17:1-28)

Proverbs - Day 18

1 Through desire a man, having separated himself, seeketh and intermeddleth with all wisdom. 2 A fool hath no delight in understanding, but that his heart may discover itself. 3 When the wicked cometh, then cometh also contempt, and with ignominy reproach. 4 The words of a man's mouth are as deep waters, and the wellspring of wisdom as a flowing brook. 5 It is not good to accept the person of the wicked, to overthrow the righteous in judgment. 6 A fool's lips enter into contention, and his mouth calleth for strokes. 7 A fool's mouth is his destruction, and his lips are the snare of his soul. 8 The words of a talebearer are as wounds, and they go down into the innermost parts of the belly. 9 He also that is slothful in his work is brother to him that is a great waster. 10 The name of the Lord is a strong tower: the righteous runneth into it, and is safe. 11 The rich man's wealth is his strong city, and as an high wall in his own conceit. 12 Before destruction the heart of man is haughty, and before honour is humility.

1 People who do not get along with others are interested only in themselves; they will disagree with what everyone else knows is right. 2 A fool does not care whether he understands a thing or not; all he wants to do is show how smart he is. 3 When a wicked person comes, contempt comes too, and with disdain, provocation . 4 A person's words can be a source of wisdom, deep as the ocean, fresh as a flowing stream. 5 It is not right to favor the guilty and keep the innocent from receiving justice. 6 When some fool starts an argument, he is asking for a beating. 7 When a fool speaks, he is ruining himself; he gets caught in the trap of his own words. 8 A slanderer's words are tasty morsels; they slide right down into the belly 9 A lazy person is as bad as someone who is destructive. 10 The name of the Lord is a strong tower, where the righteous can go and be safe. 11 The wealth of the rich is his fortified city, like a high wall, in his own imagination. 12 Before being ruined, a person's heart is proud; before being honored, a person must be humble.

13 He that answereth a matter before he heareth it, it is folly and shame unto him. 14 The spirit of a man will sustain his infirmity; but a wounded spirit who can bear? 15 The heart of the prudent getteth knowledge; and the ear of the wise seeketh knowledge. 16 A man's gift maketh room for him, and bringeth him before great men. 17 He that is first in his own cause seemeth just; but his neighbour cometh and searcheth him. 18 The lot causeth contentions to cease, and parteth between the mighty. 19 A brother offended is harder to be won than a strong city: and their contentions are like the bars of a castle. 20 A man's belly shall be satisfied with the fruit of his mouth; and with the increase of his lips shall he be filled. 21 Death and life are in the power of the tongue: and they that love it shall eat the fruit thereof. 22 Whoso findeth a wife findeth a good thing, and obtaineth favour of the Lord. 23 The poor useth intreaties; but the rich answereth roughly. 24 A man that hath friends must shew himself friendly: and there is a friend that sticketh closer than a brother. (Proverbs 18:1-24)

13 Listen before you answer. If you don't, you are being foolish and insulting. 14 A person's spirit can sustain him when ill, but a crushed spirit — who can bear it? 15 Intelligent people are always eager and ready to learn. 16 A person's gift clears his way and gives him access to the great. 17 The first person to speak in court always seems right until his opponent begins to cross-examine him. 18 If two powerful people are opposing each other in court, casting lots can settle the issue. 19 It is harder to win an offended brother than a strong city; if you quarrel with them, they will close their doors to you. 20 You will have to live with the consequences of everything you say. 21 What you say can preserve life or destroy it; so you must accept the consequences of your words. 22 Find a wife and you find a good thing; it shows that the Lord is good to you. 23 When the poor speak, they have to be polite, but when the rich answer, they are rude. 24 Some friendships do not last, but some friends are more loyal than brothers. (Proverbs 18:1-24)

Proverbs - Day 19

1 Better is the poor that walketh in his integrity, than he that is perverse in his lips, and is a fool. 2 Also, that the soul be without knowledge, it is not good; and he that hasteth with his feet sinneth. 3 The foolishness of man perverteth his way: and his heart fretteth against the Lord. 4 Wealth maketh many friends; but the poor is separated from his neighbour. 5 A false witness shall not be unpunished, and he that speaketh lies shall not escape. 6 Many will intreat the favour of the prince: and every man is a friend to him that giveth gifts. 7 All the brethren of the poor do hate him: how much more do his friends go far from him? he pursueth them with words, yet they are wanting to him. 8 He that getteth wisdom loveth his own soul: he that keepeth understanding shall find good. 9 A false witness shall not be unpunished, and he that speaketh lies shall perish. 10 Delight is not seemly for a fool; much less for a servant to have rule over princes. 11 The discretion of a man deferreth his anger; and it is his glory to pass over a transgression.

1 Better to be poor and live one's life uprightly than engage in crooked speech, for such a one is a fool. 2 Enthusiasm without knowledge is not good; impatience will get you into trouble. 3 Some people ruin themselves by their own foolish actions and then blame the Lord. 4 Rich people are always finding new friends, but the poor cannot keep the few they have. 5 If you tell lies in court, you will be punished—there will be no escape. 6 Everyone tries to gain the favor of important people; everyone claims the friendship of those who give out favors. 7 Even the relatives of a poor person have no use for him; no wonder he has no friends. No matter how hard he tries, he cannot win any. 8 Do yourself a favor and learn all you can; then remember what you learn and you will prosper. 9 No one who tells lies in court can escape punishment; he is doomed. 10 Fools should not live in luxury, and slaves should not rule over noblemen. 11 If you are sensible, you will control your temper. When someone wrongs you, it is a great virtue to ignore it.

12 The king's wrath is as the roaring of a lion; but his favour is as dew upon the grass. 13 A foolish son is the calamity of his father: and the contentions of a wife are a continual dropping. 14 House and riches are the inheritance of fathers: and a prudent wife is from the Lord. 15 Slothfulness casteth into a deep sleep; and an idle soul shall suffer hunger. 16 He that keepeth the commandment keepeth his own soul; but he that despiseth his ways shall die. 17 He that hath pity upon the poor lendeth unto the Lord; and that which he hath given will he pay him again. 18 Chasten thy son while there is hope, and let not thy soul spare for his crying. 19 A man of great wrath shall suffer punishment: for if thou deliver him, yet thou must do it again. 20 Hear counsel, and receive instruction, that thou mayest be wise in thy latter end. 21 There are many devices in a man's heart; nevertheless the counsel of the Lord, that shall stand. 22 The desire of a man is his kindness: and a poor man is better than a liar. 23 The fear of the Lord tendeth to life: and he that hath it shall abide satisfied; he shall not be visited with evil. 24 A slothful man hideth his hand in his bosom, and will not so much as bring it to his mouth again.

12 The king's anger is like the roar of a lion, but his favor is like welcome rain. 13 A son who is a fool is his father's ruin, and a nagging wife is like a leak that keeps dripping. 14 A man can inherit a house and money from his parents, but only the Lord can give him a sensible wife. 15 Go ahead and be lazy; sleep on, but you will go hungry. 16 He who keeps a commandment keeps himself safe, but he who doesn't care how he lives will die.
17 When you give to the poor, it is like lending to the Lord, and the Lord will pay you back.
18 Discipline your children while they are young enough to learn. If you don't, you are helping them destroy themselves. 19 If someone has a hot temper, let him take the consequences. If you get him out of trouble once, you will have to do it again. 20 If you listen to advice and are willing to learn, one day you will be wise. 21 People may plan all kinds of things, but the Lord's will is going to be done. 22 It is a disgrace to be greedy; poor people are better off than liars. 23 Obey the Lord and you will live a long life, content and safe from harm. 24 Some people are too lazy to put food in their own mouths.

25 Smite a scorner, and the simple will beware: and reprove one that hath understanding, and he will understand knowledge. 26 He that wasteth his father, and chaseth away his mother, is a son that causeth shame, and bringeth reproach. 27 Cease, my son, to hear the instruction that causeth to err from the words of knowledge. 28 An ungodly witness scorneth judgment: and the mouth of the wicked devoureth iniquity. 29 Judgments are prepared for scorners, and stripes for the back of fools. (Proverbs 19:1-29)

25 Arrogance should be punished, so that people who don't know any better can learn a lesson. If you are wise, you will learn when you are corrected. 26 Only a shameful, disgraceful person would mistreat his father or turn his mother away from his home. 27 My son, if you stop heeding discipline, you will stray from the principles of knowledge. 28 A worthless witness mocks at justice, and the mouth of the wicked swallows wrongdoing. 29 Judgments are in store for scorners and blows for the backs of fools. (Proverbs 19:1-29)

Proverbs - Day 20

1 Wine is a mocker, strong drink is raging: and whosoever is deceived thereby is not wise. 2 The fear of a king is as the roaring of a lion: whoso provoketh him to anger sinneth against his own soul. 3 It is an honour for a man to cease from strife: but every fool will be meddling. 4 The sluggard will not plow by reason of the cold; therefore shall he beg in harvest, and have nothing. 5 Counsel in the heart of man is like deep water; but a man of understanding will draw it out. 6 Most men will proclaim every one his own goodness: but a faithful man who can find? 7 The just man walketh in his integrity: his children are blessed after him. 8 A king that sitteth in the throne of judgment scattereth away all evil with his eyes. 9 Who can say, I have made my heart clean, I am pure from my sin? 10 Divers weights, and divers measures, both of them are alike abomination to the Lord. 11 Even a child is known by his doings, whether his work be pure, and whether it be right. 12 The hearing ear, and the seeing eye, the Lord hath made even both of them. 13 Love not sleep, lest thou come to poverty; open thine eyes, and thou shalt be satisfied with bread.

1 Wine and strong liquor makes you loud and foolish; anyone led astray by it is unwise. 2 Fear an angry king as you would a growling lion; he who makes him angry commits a life-threatening sin. 3 Any fool can start arguments; the honorable thing is to stay out of them. 4 A farmer too lazy to plow his fields at the right time will have nothing to harvest. 5 A person's thoughts are like water in a deep well, but someone with insight can draw them out. 6 Everyone talks about how loyal and faithful he is, but just try to find someone who really is! 7 Children are fortunate if they have a father who is honest and does what is right. 8 The king seated on his judgment throne can winnow out all evil with his glance. 9 Can anyone really say that his conscience is clear, that he has gotten rid of his sin? 10 The Lord hates people who use dishonest weights and measures. 11 Even children show what they are by what they do; you can tell if they are honest and good. 12 The Lord has given us eyes to see with and ears to listen with. 13 If you spend your time sleeping, you will be poor. Keep busy and you will have plenty to eat.

14 It is naught, it is naught, saith the buyer: but when he is gone his way, then he boasteth. 15 There is gold, and a multitude of rubies: but the lips of knowledge are a precious jewel. 16 Take his garment that is surety for a stranger: and take a pledge of him for a strange woman. 17 Bread of deceit is sweet to a man; but afterwards his mouth shall be filled with gravel. 18 Every purpose is established by counsel: and with good advice make war. 19 He that goeth about as a talebearer revealeth secrets: therefore meddle not with him that flattereth with his lips. 20 Whoso curseth his father or his mother, his lamp shall be put out in obscure darkness. 21 An inheritance may be gotten hastily at the beginning; but the end thereof shall not be blessed. 22 Say not thou, I will recompense evil; but wait on the Lord, and he shall save thee. 23 Divers weights are an abomination unto the Lord; and a false balance is not good. 24 Man's goings are of the Lord; how can a man then understand his own way? 25 It is a snare to the man who devoureth that which is holy, and after vows to make enquiry. 26 A wise king scattereth the wicked, and bringeth the wheel over them.

14 The customer always complains that the price is too high, but then he goes off and brags about the bargain he got. 15 If you know what you are talking about, you have something more valuable than gold or jewels. 16 Seize his clothes, because he guaranteed a stranger's loan; take them as security for that unknown woman. 17 What you get by dishonesty you may enjoy like the finest food, but sooner or later it will be like a mouthful of sand. 18 Get good advice and you will succeed; don't go charging into battle without a plan. 19 A gossip can never keep a secret. Stay away from people who talk too much. 20 If you curse your parents, your life will end like a lamp that goes out in the dark. 21 The more easily you get your wealth, the less good it will do you. 22 Don't take it on yourself to repay a wrong. Trust the Lord and he will make it right. 23 The Lord hates people who use dishonest scales and weights. 24 The Lord has determined our path; how then can anyone understand the direction his own life is taking? 25 It is a snare to dedicate a gift to God rashly and reflect on the vows only afterwards . 26 A wise king will find out who is doing wrong, and will punish him without pity.

27 The spirit of man is the candle of the Lord, searching all the inward parts of the belly. **28** Mercy and truth preserve the king: and his throne is upholden by mercy. **29** The glory of young men is their strength: and the beauty of old men is the grey head. **30** The blueness of a wound cleanseth away evil: so do stripes the inward parts of the belly. (Proverbs 20:1-30)

27 The Lord gave us mind and conscience; we cannot hide from ourselves. **28** A king will remain in power as long as his rule is honest, just, and fair. **29** We admire the strength of youth and respect the gray hair of age.
30 Sometimes it takes a painful experience to make us change our ways. (Proverbs 20:1-30)

Proverbs - Day 21

1 The king's heart is in the hand of the Lord, as the rivers of water: he turneth it whithersoever he will. 2 Every way of a man is right in his own eyes: but the Lord pondereth the hearts. 3 To do justice and judgment is more acceptable to the Lord than sacrifice. 4 An high look, and a proud heart, and the plowing of the wicked, is sin. 5 The thoughts of the diligent tend only to plenteousness; but of every one that is hasty only to want. 6 The getting of treasures by a lying tongue is a vanity tossed to and fro of them that seek death. 7 The robbery of the wicked shall destroy them; because they refuse to do judgment. 8 The way of man is froward and strange: but as for the pure, his work is right. 9 It is better to dwell in a corner of the housetop, than with a brawling woman in a wide house. 10 The soul of the wicked desireth evil: his neighbour findeth no favour in his eyes. 11 When the scorner is punished, the simple is made wise: and when the wise is instructed, he receiveth knowledge. 12 The righteous man wisely considereth the house of the wicked: but God overthroweth the wicked for their wickedness.

1 The Lord controls the mind of a king as easily as he directs the course of a stream. 2 You may think that everything you do is right, but remember that the Lord judges your motives. 3 Do what is right and fair; that pleases the Lord more than bringing him sacrifices. 4 Wicked people are controlled by their conceit and arrogance, and this is sinful. 5 Plan carefully and you will have plenty; if you act too quickly, you will never have enough. 6 The riches you get by dishonesty soon disappear, but not before they lead you into the jaws of death. 7 The wicked are doomed by their own violence; they refuse to do what is right. 8 Guilty people walk a crooked path; the innocent do what is right. 9 Better to live on the roof than share the house with a nagging wife. 10 The wicked is set on evil; he doesn't pity even his neighbor. 11 When someone who is conceited gets his punishment, even an unthinking person learns a lesson. One who is wise will learn from what he is taught. 12 God, the righteous one, knows what goes on in the homes of the wicked, and he will bring the wicked down to ruin.

13 Whoso stoppeth his ears at the cry of the poor, he also shall cry himself, but shall not be heard. 14 A gift in secret pacifieth anger: and a reward in the bosom strong wrath. 15 It is joy to the just to do judgment: but destruction shall be to the workers of iniquity. 16 The man that wandereth out of the way of understanding shall remain in the congregation of the dead. 17 He that loveth pleasure shall be a poor man: he that loveth wine and oil shall not be rich. 18 The wicked shall be a ransom for the righteous, and the transgressor for the upright. 19 It is better to dwell in the wilderness, than with a contentious and an angry woman. 20 There is treasure to be desired and oil in the dwelling of the wise; but a foolish man spendeth it up. 21 He that followeth after righteousness and mercy findeth life, righteousness, and honour. 22 A wise man scaleth the city of the mighty, and casteth down the strength of the confidence thereof. 23 Whoso keepeth his mouth and his tongue keepeth his soul from troubles. 24 Proud and haughty scorner is his name, who dealeth in proud wrath. 25 The desire of the slothful killeth him; for his hands refuse to labour. 26 He coveteth greedily all the day long: but the righteous giveth and spareth not.

13 If you refuse to listen to the cry of the poor, your own cry for help will not be heard. 14 If someone is angry with you, a gift given secretly will calm him down. 15 When justice is done, good people are happy, but evil people are brought to despair. 16 Death is waiting for anyone who wanders away from good sense. 17 Indulging in luxuries, wine, and rich food will never make you wealthy. 18 The wicked bring on themselves the suffering they try to cause good people. 19 Better to live out in the desert than with a nagging, complaining wife. 20 In the home of the wise are fine treasures and oil, but foolish people spend their money as fast as they get it. 21 Be kind and honest and you will live a long life; others will respect you and treat you fairly. 22 A shrewd general can take a city defended by strong men, and destroy the walls they relied on. 23 If you want to stay out of trouble, be careful what you say. 24 Show me a conceited person and I will show you someone who is arrogant, proud, and inconsiderate. 25 Lazy people who refuse to work are only killing themselves; 26 all they do is think about what they would like to have. The righteous, however, can give, and give generously.

27 The sacrifice of the wicked is abomination: how much more, when he bringeth it with a wicked mind? 28 A false witness shall perish: but the man that heareth speaketh constantly. 29 A wicked man hardeneth his face: but as for the upright, he directeth his way. 30 There is no wisdom nor understanding nor counsel against the Lord. 31 The horse is prepared against the day of battle: but safety is of the Lord. (Proverbs 21:1-31)

27 The Lord hates it when wicked people offer him sacrifices, especially if they do it from evil motives. 28 The testimony of a liar is not believed, but the word of someone who thinks matters through is accepted. 29 Righteous people are sure of themselves; the wicked have to pretend as best they can. 30 Human wisdom, brilliance, insight—they are of no help if the Lord is against you. 31 You can get horses ready for battle, but it is the Lord who gives victory. (Proverbs 21:1-31)

Proverbs - Day 22

1 A good name is rather to be chosen than great riches, and loving favour rather than silver and gold. 2 The rich and poor meet together: the Lord is the maker of them all. 3 A prudent man foreseeth the evil, and hideth himself: but the simple pass on, and are punished. 4 By humility and the fear of the Lord are riches, and honour, and life. 5 Thorns and snares are in the way of the froward: he that doth keep his soul shall be far from them. 6 Train up a child in the way he should go: and when he is old, he will not depart from it. 7 The rich ruleth over the poor, and the borrower is servant to the lender. 8 He that soweth iniquity shall reap vanity: and the rod of his anger shall fail. 9 He that hath a bountiful eye shall be blessed; for he giveth of his bread to the poor. 10 Cast out the scorner, and contention shall go out; yea, strife and reproach shall cease. 11 He that loveth pureness of heart, for the grace of his lips the king shall be his friend. 12 The eyes of the Lord preserve knowledge, and he overthroweth the words of the transgressor. 13 The slothful man saith, There is a lion without, I shall be slain in the streets.

1 If you have to choose between a good reputation and great wealth, choose a good reputation. 2 The rich and the poor have this in common: the Lord made them both. 3 Sensible people will see trouble coming and avoid it, but an unthinking person will walk right into it and regret it later. 4 Obey the Lord, be humble, and you will get riches, honor, and a long life. 5 If you love your life, stay away from the traps that catch the wicked along the way. 6 Teach children how they should live, and they will remember it all their life. 7 Poor people are slaves of the rich. Borrow money and you are the lender's slave. 8 If you plant the seeds of injustice, disaster will spring up, and your oppression of others will end. 9 Be generous and share your food with the poor. You will be blessed for it. 10 Get rid of a conceited person, and then there will be no more arguments, quarreling, or name-calling. 11 If you love purity of heart and graciousness of speech, the king will be your friend. 12 The Lord sees to it that truth is kept safe by disproving the words of liars. 13 Lazy people stay at home; they say a lion might get them if they go outside.

14 The mouth of strange women is a deep pit: he that is abhorred of the Lord shall fall therein. 15 Foolishness is bound in the heart of a child; but the rod of correction shall drive it far from him. 16 He that oppresseth the poor to increase his riches, and he that giveth to the rich, shall surely come to want. 17 Bow down thine ear, and hear the words of the wise, and apply thine heart unto my knowledge. 18 For it is a pleasant thing if thou keep them within thee; they shall withal be fitted in thy lips. 19 That thy trust may be in the Lord, I have made known to thee this day, even to thee. 20 Have not I written to thee excellent things in counsels and knowledge, 21 That I might make thee know the certainty of the words of truth; that thou mightest answer the words of truth to them that send unto thee? 22 Rob not the poor, because he is poor: neither oppress the afflicted in the gate: 23 For the Lord will plead their cause, and spoil the soul of those that spoiled them. 24 Make no friendship with an angry man; and with a furious man thou shalt not go: 25 Lest thou learn his ways, and get a snare to thy soul. 26 Be not thou one of them that strike hands, or of them that are sureties for debts.

14 The mouth of an adulteress is a deep pit; the man with whom the Lord is angry falls into it. 15 Children just naturally do silly, careless things, but a good spanking will teach them how to behave. 16 If you make gifts to rich people or oppress the poor to get rich, you will become poor yourself. 17 Pay attention, and listen to the words of the wise; apply your heart to my knowledge; 18 for it is pleasant to keep them deep within you; have all of them ready on your lips. 19 I want your trust to be in the Lord; this is why I'm instructing you about them today. 20 I have written you worthwhile things full of good counsel and knowledge 21 and will teach you what the truth really is. Then when you are sent to find it out, you will bring back the right answer. 22 Don't take advantage of the poor just because you can; don't take advantage of those who stand helpless in court. 23 The Lord will argue their case for them and threaten the life of anyone who threatens theirs. 24 Don't make friends with people who have hot, violent tempers. 25 You might learn their habits and not be able to change. 26 Don't promise to be responsible for someone else's debts.

27 If thou hast nothing to pay, why should he take away thy bed from under thee? 28 Remove not the ancient landmark, which thy fathers have set. 29 Seest thou a man diligent in his business? he shall stand before kings; he shall not stand before mean men. (Proverbs 22:1-29)

27 If you should be unable to pay, they will take away even your bed. 28 Never move an old property line that your ancestors established. 29 Show me someone who does a good job, and I will show you someone who is better than most and worthy of the company of kings. (Proverbs 22:1-29)

Proverbs - Day 23

1 When thou sittest to eat with a ruler, consider diligently what is before thee: 2 And put a knife to thy throat, if thou be a man given to appetite. 3 Be not desirous of his dainties: for they are deceitful meat. 4 Labour not to be rich: cease from thine own wisdom. 5 Wilt thou set thine eyes upon that which is not? for riches certainly make themselves wings; they fly away as an eagle toward heaven. 6 Eat thou not the bread of him that hath an evil eye, neither desire thou his dainty meats: 7 For as he thinketh in his heart, so is he: Eat and drink, saith he to thee; but his heart is not with thee. 8 The morsel which thou hast eaten shalt thou vomit up, and lose thy sweet words. 9 Speak not in the ears of a fool: for he will despise the wisdom of thy words. 10 Remove not the old landmark; and enter not into the fields of the fatherless: 11 For their redeemer is mighty; he shall plead their cause with thee. 12 Apply thine heart unto instruction, and thine ears to the words of knowledge. 13 Withhold not correction from the child: for if thou beatest him with the rod, he shall not die. 14 Thou shalt beat him with the rod, and shalt deliver his soul from hell.

1 When you sit down to eat with someone important, keep in mind who he is. 2 If you have a big appetite, restrain yourself. 3 Don't be greedy for the fine food he serves; he may be trying to trick you. 4 Be wise enough not to wear yourself out trying to get rich. 5 Your money can be gone in a flash, as if it had grown wings and flown away like an eagle. 6 Don't eat at the table of a stingy person or be greedy for the fine food he serves. 7 "Come on and have some more," he says, but he doesn't mean it. What he thinks is what he really is. 8 You will vomit up what you have eaten, and all your flattery will be wasted. 9 Don't try to talk sense to a fool; he can't appreciate it. 10 Never move an old property line or take over land owned by orphans. 11 The Lord is their powerful defender, and he will argue their case against you. 12 Pay attention to your teacher and learn all you can. 13 Don't hesitate to discipline children. A good spanking won't kill them. 14 As a matter of fact, it may save their lives.

15 My son, if thine heart be wise, my heart shall rejoice, even mine. 16 Yea, my reins shall rejoice, when thy lips speak right things. 17 Let not thine heart envy sinners: but be thou in the fear of the Lord all the day long. 18 For surely there is an end; and thine expectation shall not be cut off. 19 Hear thou, my son, and be wise, and guide thine heart in the way. 20 Be not among winebibbers; among riotous eaters of flesh: 21 For the drunkard and the glutton shall come to poverty: and drowsiness shall clothe a man with rags. 22 Hearken unto thy father that begat thee, and despise not thy mother when she is old. 23 Buy the truth, and sell it not; also wisdom, and instruction, and understanding. 24 The father of the righteous shall greatly rejoice: and he that begetteth a wise child shall have joy of him. 25 Thy father and thy mother shall be glad, and she that bare thee shall rejoice. 26 My son, give me thine heart, and let thine eyes observe my ways. 27 For a whore is a deep ditch; and a strange woman is a narrow pit. 28 She also lieth in wait as for a prey, and increaseth the transgressors among men.

15 My child, if you become wise, I will be very happy. 16 I will be proud when I hear you speaking words of wisdom. 17 Don't be envious of sinful people; let reverence for the Lord be the concern of your life. 18 If it is, you have a bright future. 19 Listen, my child, be wise and give serious thought to the way you live. 20 Don't associate with people who drink too much wine or stuff themselves with food. 21 Drunkards and gluttons will be reduced to poverty. If all you do is eat and sleep, you will soon be wearing rags. 22 Listen to your father; without him you would not exist. When your mother is old, show her your appreciation. 23 Truth, wisdom, learning, and good sense—these are worth paying for, but too valuable for you to sell. 24 A righteous person's parents have good reason to be happy. You can take pride in a wise child. 25 Let your father and mother be proud of you; give your mother that happiness. 26 Pay close attention, son, and let my life be your example. 27 Prostitutes and immoral women are a deadly trap. 28 They wait for you like robbers and cause many men to be unfaithful.

29 Who hath woe? who hath sorrow? who hath contentions? who hath babbling? who hath wounds without cause? who hath redness of eyes? 30 They that tarry long at the wine; they that go to seek mixed wine. 31 Look not thou upon the wine when it is red, when it giveth his colour in the cup, when it moveth itself aright. 32 At the last it biteth like a serpent, and stingeth like an adder. 33 Thine eyes shall behold strange women, and thine heart shall utter perverse things. 34 Yea, thou shalt be as he that lieth down in the midst of the sea, or as he that lieth upon the top of a mast. 35 They have stricken me, shalt thou say, and I was not sick; they have beaten me, and I felt it not: when shall I awake? I will seek it yet again. (Proverbs 23:1-35)

29-30 Show me people who drink too much, who have to try out fancy drinks, and I will show you people who are miserable and sorry for themselves, always causing trouble and always complaining. Their eyes are bloodshot, and they have bruises that could have been avoided. 31 Don't let wine tempt you, even though it is rich red, and it sparkles in the cup, and it goes down smoothly. 32 The next morning you will feel as if you had been bitten by a poisonous snake. 33 Weird sights will appear before your eyes, and you will not be able to think or speak clearly. 34 You will feel as if you were out on the ocean, seasick, swinging high up in the rigging of a tossing ship. 35 "I must have been hit," you will say; "I must have been beaten up, but I don't remember it. Why can't I wake up? I'll go get another drink." (Proverbs 23:1-35)

Proverbs - Day 24

1 Be not thou envious against evil men, neither desire to be with them. 2 For their heart studieth destruction, and their lips talk of mischief. 3 Through wisdom is an house builded; and by understanding it is established: 4 And by knowledge shall the chambers be filled with all precious and pleasant riches. 5 A wise man is strong; yea, a man of knowledge increaseth strength. 6 For by wise counsel thou shalt make thy war: and in multitude of counsellors there is safety. 7 Wisdom is too high for a fool: he openeth not his mouth in the gate. 8 He that deviseth to do evil shall be called a mischievous person. 9 The thought of foolishness is sin: and the scorner is an abomination to men. 10 If thou faint in the day of adversity, thy strength is small. 11 If thou forbear to deliver them that are drawn unto death, and those that are ready to be slain; 12 If thou sayest, Behold, we knew it not; doth not he that pondereth the heart consider it? and he that keepeth thy soul, doth not he know it? and shall not he render to every man according to his works?

1 Don't be envious of evil people, and don't try to make friends with them. 2 Causing trouble is all they ever think about; every time they open their mouth someone is going to be hurt. 3 Homes are built on the foundation of wisdom and understanding. 4 Where there is knowledge, the rooms are furnished with valuable, beautiful things. 5 Being wise is better than being strong; yes, knowledge is more important than strength. 6 After all, you must make careful plans before you fight a battle, and the more good advice you get, the more likely you are to win. 7 Wise sayings are too deep for foolish people to understand. They have nothing to say when important matters are being discussed. 8 If you are always planning evil, you will earn a reputation as a troublemaker. 9 Any scheme a fool thinks up is sinful. People hate a person who has nothing but scorn for others. 10 If you are weak in a crisis, you are weak indeed. 11 Don't hesitate to rescue someone who is about to be executed unjustly. 12 You may say that it is none of your business, but God knows and judges your motives. He keeps watch on you; he knows. And he will reward you according to what you do.

13 My son, eat thou honey, because it is good; and the honeycomb, which is sweet to thy taste: 14 So shall the knowledge of wisdom be unto thy soul: when thou hast found it, then there shall be a reward, and thy expectation shall not be cut off. 15 Lay not wait, O wicked man, against the dwelling of the righteous; spoil not his resting place: 16 For a just man falleth seven times, and riseth up again: but the wicked shall fall into mischief. 17 Rejoice not when thine enemy falleth, and let not thine heart be glad when he stumbleth: 18 Lest the Lord see it, and it displease him, and he turn away his wrath from him. 19 Fret not thyself because of evil men, neither be thou envious at the wicked: 20 For there shall be no reward to the evil man; the candle of the wicked shall be put out. 21 My son, fear thou the Lord and the king: and meddle not with them that are given to change: 22 For their calamity shall rise suddenly; and who knoweth the ruin of them both? 23 These things also belong to the wise. It is not good to have respect of persons in judgment. 24 He that saith unto the wicked, Thou are righteous; him shall the people curse, nations shall abhor him: 25 But to them that rebuke him shall be delight, and a good blessing shall come upon them.

13 My child, eat honey; it is good. And just as honey from the comb is sweet on your tongue, 14 you may be sure that wisdom is good for the soul. Get wisdom and you have a bright future. 15 Don't be like the wicked who scheme to rob honest people or to take away their homes. 16 No matter how often honest people fall, they always get up again; but disaster destroys the wicked. 17 Don't be glad when your enemies meet disaster, and don't rejoice when they stumble. 18 The Lord will know if you are gloating, and he will not like it; and then maybe he won't punish them. 19 Don't let evil people worry you; don't be envious of them. 20 A wicked person has no future—nothing to look forward to. 21 Have reverence for the Lord, my child, and honor the king. Have nothing to do with people who rebel against them; 22 such people could be ruined in a moment. Do you realize the disaster that God or the king can cause? 23 The wise have also said these things: It is wrong for judges to be prejudiced. 24 If they pronounce a guilty person innocent, they will be cursed and hated by everyone. 25 Judges who punish the guilty, however, will be prosperous and enjoy a good reputation.

26 Every man shall kiss his lips that giveth a right answer. 27 Prepare thy work without, and make it fit for thyself in the field; and afterwards build thine house. 28 Be not a witness against thy neighbour without cause; and deceive not with thy lips. 29 Say not, I will do so to him as he hath done to me: I will render to the man according to his work. 30 I went by the field of the slothful, and by the vineyard of the man void of understanding; 31 And, lo, it was all grown over with thorns, and nettles had covered the face thereof, and the stone wall thereof was broken down. 32 Then I saw, and considered it well: I looked upon it, and received instruction. 33 Yet a little sleep, a little slumber, a little folding of the hands to sleep: 34 So shall thy poverty come as one that travelleth; and thy want as an armed man. **(Proverbs 24:1-34)**

26 An honest answer is a sign of true friendship. 27 Don't build your house and establish a home until your fields are ready, and you are sure that you can earn a living. 28 Don't give evidence against others without good reason, or say misleading things about them. 29 Don't say, "I'll do to them just what they did to me! I'll get even with them!" 30 I walked through the fields and vineyards of a lazy, foolish person. 31 They were full of thorn bushes and overgrown with weeds. The stone wall around them had fallen down. 32 I looked at this, thought about it, and learned a lesson from it: 33 Go ahead and take your nap; go ahead and sleep. Fold your hands and rest awhile, 34 but while you are asleep, poverty will attack you like an armed robber. **(Proverbs 24:1-34)**

Proverbs - Day 25

1 These are also proverbs of Solomon, which the men of Hezekiah king of Judah copied out. 2 It is the glory of God to conceal a thing: but the honour of kings is to search out a matter. 3 The heaven for height, and the earth for depth, and the heart of kings is unsearchable. 4 Take away the dross from the silver, and there shall come forth a vessel for the finer. 5 Take away the wicked from before the king, and his throne shall be established in righteousness. 6 Put not forth thyself in the presence of the king, and stand not in the place of great men: 7 For better it is that it be said unto thee, Come up hither; than that thou shouldest be put lower in the presence of the prince whom thine eyes have seen. 8 Go not forth hastily to strive, lest thou know not what to do in the end thereof, when thy neighbour hath put thee to shame. 9 Debate thy cause with thy neighbour himself; and discover not a secret to another: 10 Lest he that heareth it put thee to shame, and thine infamy turn not away. 11 A word fitly spoken is like apples of gold in pictures of silver.

1 Here are more of Solomon's proverbs, copied by scribes at the court of King Hezekiah of Judah. 2 We honor God for what he conceals; we honor kings for what they explain. 3 You never know what a king is thinking; his thoughts are beyond us, like the heights of the sky or the depths of the ocean. 4 Take the impurities out of silver and the artist can produce a thing of beauty. 5 Keep evil advisers away from the king and his government will be known for its justice. 6 When you stand before the king, don't try to impress him and pretend to be important. 7 It is better to be asked to take a higher position than to be told to give your place to someone more important. 8 Don't be too quick to go to court about something you have seen. If another witness later proves you wrong, what will you do then? 9 If you and your neighbor have a difference of opinion, settle it between yourselves and do not reveal any secrets. 10 Otherwise everyone will learn that you can't keep a secret, and you will never live down the shame. 11 A word appropriately spoken is like a design of gold, set in silver.

12 As an earring of gold, and an ornament of fine gold, so is a wise reprover upon an obedient ear. 13 As the cold of snow in the time of harvest, so is a faithful messenger to them that send him: for he refresheth the soul of his masters. 14 Whoso boasteth himself of a false gift is like clouds and wind without rain. 15 By long forbearing is a prince persuaded, and a soft tongue breaketh the bone. 16 Hast thou found honey? eat so much as is sufficient for thee, lest thou be filled therewith, and vomit it. 17 Withdraw thy foot from thy neighbour's house; lest he be weary of thee, and so hate thee. 18 A man that beareth false witness against his neighbour is a maul, and a sword, and a sharp arrow. 19 Confidence in an unfaithful man in time of trouble is like a broken tooth, and a foot out of joint. 20 As he that taketh away a garment in cold weather, and as vinegar upon nitre, so is he that singeth songs to an heavy heart. 21 If thine enemy be hungry, give him bread to eat; and if he be thirsty, give him water to drink: 22 For thou shalt heap coals of fire upon his head, and the Lord shall reward thee. 23 The north wind driveth away rain: so doth an angry countenance a backbiting tongue.

12 A warning given by an experienced person to someone willing to listen is more valuable than gold rings or jewelry made of the finest gold. 13 A reliable messenger is refreshing to the one who sends him, like cold water in the heat of harvest time. 14 People who promise things that they never give are like clouds and wind that bring no rain. 15 Patient persuasion can break down the strongest resistance and can even convince rulers. 16 Never eat more honey than you need; too much may make you vomit. 17 Don't visit your neighbors too often; they may get tired of you and come to hate you. 18 A false accusation is as deadly as a sword, a club, or a sharp arrow. 19 Depending on an unreliable person in a crisis is like trying to chew with a loose tooth or walk with a crippled foot. 20 Singing to a person who is depressed is like taking off a person's clothes on a cold day or like rubbing salt in a wound. 21 If your enemies are hungry, feed them; if they are thirsty, give them a drink. 22 You will make them burn with shame, and the Lord will reward you. 23 Gossip brings anger just as surely as the north wind brings rain.

24 It is better to dwell in the corner of the housetop, than with a brawling woman and in a wide house. 25 As cold waters to a thirsty soul, so is good news from a far country. 26 A righteous man falling down before the wicked is as a troubled fountain, and a corrupt spring. 27 It is not good to eat much honey: so for men to search their own glory is not glory. 28 He that hath no rule over his own spirit is like a city that is broken down, and without walls. (Proverbs 25:1-28)

24 Better to live on the roof than share the house with a nagging wife. 25 Finally hearing good news from a distant land is like a drink of cold water when you are dry and thirsty. 26 A good person who gives in to someone who is evil reminds you of a polluted spring or a poisoned well. 27 Too much honey is bad for you, and so is trying to win too much praise. 28 If you cannot control your anger, you are as helpless as a city without walls, open to attack. (Proverbs 25:1-28)

Proverbs - Day 26

1 As snow in summer, and as rain in harvest, so honour is not seemly for a fool. 2 As the bird by wandering, as the swallow by flying, so the curse causeless shall not come. 3 A whip for the horse, a bridle for the ass, and a rod for the fool's back. 4 Answer not a fool according to his folly, lest thou also be like unto him. 5 Answer a fool according to his folly, lest he be wise in his own conceit. 6 He that sendeth a message by the hand of a fool cutteth off the feet, and drinketh damage. 7 The legs of the lame are not equal: so is a parable in the mouth of fools. 8 As he that bindeth a stone in a sling, so is he that giveth honour to a fool. 9 As a thorn goeth up into the hand of a drunkard, so is a parable in the mouths of fools. 10 The great God that formed all things both rewardeth the fool, and rewardeth transgressors. 11 As a dog returneth to his vomit, so a fool returneth to his folly. 12 Seest thou a man wise in his own conceit? there is more hope of a fool than of him. 13 The slothful man saith, There is a lion in the way; a lion is in the streets. 14 As the door turneth upon his hinges, so doth the slothful upon his bed.

1 Praise for a fool is out of place, like snow in summer or rain at harvest time. 2 Curses cannot hurt you unless you deserve them. They are like birds that fly by and never light. 3 You have to whip a horse, you have to bridle a donkey, and you have to beat a fool. 4 Don't answer a fool in terms of his folly, or you will be descending to his level; 5 but answer a fool as his folly deserves, so that he won't think he is wise. 6 If you let a fool deliver a message, you might as well cut off your own feet; you are asking for trouble. 7 The legs of the disabled hang limp and useless; likewise a proverb in the mouth of a fool. 8 Praising someone who is foolish makes as much sense as tying a stone in a sling. 9 A fool quoting a wise saying reminds you of a drunk trying to pick a thorn out of his hand. 10 A master can make anything, but hiring a fool is like hiring some passer-by. 11 Just as a dog returns to his vomit, a fool repeats his folly. 12 Do you see someone who thinks himself wise? There is more hope for a fool than for him! 13 The lazy person says, "There's a lion in the streets! A lion is roaming loose out there! 14 Lazy people turn over in bed. They get no farther than a door swinging on its hinges.

15 The slothful hideth his hand in his bosom; it grieveth him to bring it again to his mouth. 16 The sluggard is wiser in his own conceit than seven men that can render a reason. 17 He that passeth by, and meddleth with strife belonging not to him, is like one that taketh a dog by the ears. 18 As a mad man who casteth firebrands, arrows, and death, 19 So is the man that deceiveth his neighbour, and saith, Am not I in sport? 20 Where no wood is, there the fire goeth out: so where there is no talebearer, the strife ceaseth. 21 As coals are to burning coals, and wood to fire; so is a contentious man to kindle strife. 22 The words of a talebearer are as wounds, and they go down into the innermost parts of the belly. 23 Burning lips and a wicked heart are like a potsherd covered with silver dross. 24 He that hateth dissembleth with his lips, and layeth up deceit within him; 25 When he speaketh fair, believe him not: for there are seven abominations in his heart. 26 Whose hatred is covered by deceit, his wickedness shall be shewed before the whole congregation. 27 Whoso diggeth a pit shall fall therein: and he that rolleth a stone, it will return upon him. 28 A lying tongue hateth those that are afflicted by it; and a flattering mouth worketh ruin.

15 Some people are too lazy to put food in their own mouths. 16 A lazy person will think he is smarter than seven men who can give good reasons for their opinions. 17 Getting involved in an argument that is none of your business is like going down the street and grabbing a dog by the ears. 18-19 Someone who tricks someone else and then claims that he was only joking is like a crazy person playing with a deadly weapon. 20 Without wood, a fire goes out; without gossip, quarreling stops. 21 Charcoal keeps the embers glowing, wood keeps the fire burning, and troublemakers keep arguments alive. 22 A slanderer's words are tasty morsels; they slide right down into the belly! 23 Insincere talk that hides what you are really thinking is like a fine glaze on a cheap clay pot. 24 A hypocrite hides hate behind flattering words. 25 They may sound fine, but don't believe him, because his heart is filled to the brim with hate. 26 He may disguise his hatred, but everyone will see the evil things he does. 27 People who set traps for others get caught themselves. People who start landslides get crushed. 28 You have to hate someone to want to hurt him with lies. Insincere talk brings nothing but ruin.

(Proverbs 26:1-28)

Proverbs - Day 27

1 Boast not thyself of to morrow; for thou knowest not what a day may bring forth. 2 Let another man praise thee, and not thine own mouth; a stranger, and not thine own lips. 3 A stone is heavy, and the sand weighty; but a fool's wrath is heavier than them both. 4 Wrath is cruel, and anger is outrageous; but who is able to stand before envy? 5 Open rebuke is better than secret love. 6 Faithful are the wounds of a friend; but the kisses of an enemy are deceitful. 7 The full soul loatheth an honeycomb; but to the hungry soul every bitter thing is sweet. 8 As a bird that wandereth from her nest, so is a man that wandereth from his place. 9 Ointment and perfume rejoice the heart: so doth the sweetness of a man's friend by hearty counsel. 10 Thine own friend, and thy father's friend, forsake not; neither go into thy brother's house in the day of thy calamity: for better is a neighbour that is near than a brother far off. 11 My son, be wise, and make my heart glad, that I may answer him that reproacheth me. 12 A prudent man foreseeth the evil, and hideth himself; but the simple pass on, and are punished.

1 Never boast about tomorrow. You don't know what will happen between now and then. 2 Let other people praise you—even strangers; never do it yourself. 3 The weight of stone and sand is nothing compared to the trouble that stupidity can cause. 4 Anger is cruel and destructive, but it is nothing compared to jealousy. 5 Better to correct someone openly than to let him think you don't care for him at all. 6 Friends mean well, even when they hurt you. But when an enemy puts his arm around your shoulder—watch out! 7 When you are full, you will refuse honey, but when you are hungry, even bitter food tastes sweet. 8 Anyone away from home is like a bird away from its nest. 9 Perfume and incense make the heart glad, [also] friendship sweet with advice from the heart. 10 Do not forget your friends or your father's friends. If you are in trouble, don't ask a relative for help; a nearby neighbor can help you more than relatives who are far away. 11 Be wise, my child, and I will be happy; I will have an answer for anyone who criticizes me. 12 Sensible people will see trouble coming and avoid it, but an unthinking person will walk right into it and regret it later.

13 Take his garment that is surety for a stranger, and take a pledge of him for a strange woman. 14 He that blesseth his friend with a loud voice, rising early in the morning, it shall be counted a curse to him. 15 A continual dropping in a very rainy day and a contentious woman are alike. 16 Whosoever hideth her hideth the wind, and the ointment of his right hand, which bewrayeth itself. 17 Iron sharpeneth iron; so a man sharpeneth the countenance of his friend. 18 Whoso keepeth the fig tree shall eat the fruit thereof: so he that waiteth on his master shall be honoured. 19 As in water face answereth to face, so the heart of man to man. 20 Hell and destruction are never full; so the eyes of man are never satisfied. 21 As the fining pot for silver, and the furnace for gold; so is a man to his praise. 22 Though thou shouldest bray a fool in a mortar among wheat with a pestle, yet will not his foolishness depart from him. 23 Be thou diligent to know the state of thy flocks, and look well to thy herds. 24 For riches are not for ever: and doth the crown endure to every generation? 25 The hay appeareth, and the tender grass sheweth itself, and herbs of the mountains are gathered.

13 Seize his clothes because he guaranteed a stranger's loan; take them as security for that unknown woman. 14 You might as well curse your friends as wake them up early in the morning with a loud greeting. 15 A leak that keeps dripping on a rainy day and the nagging of a wife are the same — 16 whoever can restrain her can restrain the wind or keep perfume on his hand from making itself known. 17 Just as iron sharpens iron, a person sharpens the character of his friend. 18 Take care of a fig tree and you will have figs to eat. Servants who take care of their master will be honored. 19 It is your own face that you see reflected in the water and it is your own self that you see in your heart. 20 Human desires are like the world of the dead—there is always room for more. 21 Fire tests gold and silver; a person's reputation can also be tested. 22 Even if you beat fools half to death, you still can't beat their foolishness out of them. 23 Look after your sheep and cattle as carefully as you can, 24 because wealth is not permanent. Not even nations last forever. 25 You cut the hay and then cut the grass on the hillsides while the next crop of hay is growing.

26 The lambs are for thy clothing, and the goats are the price of the field. 27 And thou shalt have goats' milk enough for thy food, for the food of thy household, and for the maintenance for thy maidens. (Proverbs 27:1-27)

26 You can make clothes from the wool of your sheep and buy land with the money you get from selling some of your goats. 27 The rest of the goats will provide milk for you and your family, and for your servant women as well. (Proverbs 27:1-27)

Proverbs - Day 28

1 The wicked flee when no man pursueth: but the righteous are bold as a lion. 2 For the transgression of a land many are the princes thereof: but by a man of understanding and knowledge the state thereof shall be prolonged. 3 A poor man that oppresseth the poor is like a sweeping rain which leaveth no food. 4 They that forsake the law praise the wicked: but such as keep the law contend with them. 5 Evil men understand not judgment: but they that seek the Lord understand all things. 6 Better is the poor that walketh in his uprightness, than he that is perverse in his ways, though he be rich. 7 Whoso keepeth the law is a wise son: but he that is a companion of riotous men shameth his father. 8 He that by usury and unjust gain increaseth his substance, he shall gather it for him that will pity the poor. 9 He that turneth away his ear from hearing the law, even his prayer shall be abomination. 10 Whoso causeth the righteous to go astray in an evil way, he shall fall himself into his own pit: but the upright shall have good things in possession.

1 The wicked run when no one is chasing them, but an honest person is as brave as a lion. 2 When a nation sins, it will have one ruler after another. But a nation will be strong and endure when it has intelligent, sensible leaders. 3 Someone in authority who oppresses poor people is like a driving rain that destroys the crops. 4 If you have no regard for the law, you are on the side of the wicked; but if you obey it, you are against them. 5 Evil people do not know what justice is, but those who worship the Lord understand it well. 6 Better to be poor and honest than rich and dishonest. 7 Young people who obey the law are intelligent. Those who make friends with good-for-nothings are a disgrace to their parents. 8 If you get rich by charging interest and taking advantage of people, your wealth will go to someone who is kind to the poor. 9 If you do not obey the law, God will find your prayers too hateful to hear. 10 Whoever causes the honest to pursue evil ways will himself fall into his own pit, but the purehearted will inherit good.

11 The rich man is wise in his own conceit; but the poor that hath understanding searcheth him out. 12 When righteous men do rejoice, there is great glory: but when the wicked rise, a man is hidden. 13 He that covereth his sins shall not prosper: but whoso confesseth and forsaketh them shall have mercy. 14 Happy is the man that feareth alway: but he that hardeneth his heart shall fall into mischief. 15 As a roaring lion, and a ranging bear; so is a wicked ruler over the poor people. 16 The prince that wanteth understanding is also a great oppressor: but he that hateth covetousness shall prolong his days. 17 A man that doeth violence to the blood of any person shall flee to the pit; let no man stay him. 18 Whoso walketh uprightly shall be saved: but he that is perverse in his ways shall fall at once. 19 He that tilleth his land shall have plenty of bread: but he that followeth after vain persons shall have poverty enough. 20 A faithful man shall abound with blessings: but he that maketh haste to be rich shall not be innocent. 21 To have respect of persons is not good: for for a piece of bread that man will transgress. 22 He that hasteth to be rich hath an evil eye, and considereth not that poverty shall come upon him.

11 Rich people always think they are wise, but a poor person who has insight into character knows better. 12 When good people come to power, everybody celebrates, but when bad people rule, people stay in hiding. 13 You will never succeed in life if you try to hide your sins. Confess them and give them up; then God will show mercy to you. 14 Always obey the Lord and you will be happy. If you are stubborn, you will be ruined. 15 Poor people are helpless against a wicked ruler; he is as dangerous as a growling lion or a prowling bear. 16 A ruler without good sense will be a cruel tyrant. One who hates dishonesty will rule a long time. 17 Let a man weighed down with anyone's blood flee to a pit; give him no support. 18 Be honest and you will be safe. If you are dishonest, you will suddenly fall. 19 A hardworking farmer has plenty to eat. People who waste time will always be poor. 20 Honest people will lead a full, happy life. But if you are in a hurry to get rich, you are going to be punished. 21 Prejudice is wrong. But some judges will do wrong to get even the smallest bribe. 22 Selfish people are in such a hurry to get rich that they do not know when poverty is about to strike.

23 He that rebuketh a man afterwards shall find more favour than he that flattereth with the tongue. 24 Whoso robbeth his father or his mother, and saith, It is no transgression; the same is the companion of a destroyer. 25 He that is of a proud heart stirreth up strife: but he that putteth his trust in the Lord shall be made fat. 26 He that trusteth in his own heart is a fool: but whoso walketh wisely, he shall be delivered. 27 He that giveth unto the poor shall not lack: but he that hideth his eyes shall have many a curse. 28 When the wicked rise, men hide themselves: but when they perish, the righteous increase. (Proverbs 28:1-28)

23 Correct someone, and afterward he will appreciate it more than flattery. 24 Anyone who thinks it isn't wrong to steal from his parents is no better than a common thief. 25 Selfishness only causes trouble. You are much better off to trust the Lord. 26 It is foolish to follow your own opinions. Be safe, and follow the teachings of wiser people. 27 Give to the poor and you will never be in need. If you close your eyes to the poor, many people will curse you. 28 People stay in hiding when the wicked come to power. But when they fall from power, the righteous will rule again. (Proverbs 28:1-28)

Proverbs - Day 29

1 He, that being often reproved hardeneth his neck, shall suddenly be destroyed, and that without remedy. 2 When the righteous are in authority, the people rejoice: but when the wicked beareth rule, the people mourn. 3 Whoso loveth wisdom rejoiceth his father: but he that keepeth company with harlots spendeth his substance. 4 The king by judgment establisheth the land: but he that receiveth gifts overthroweth it. 5 A man that flattereth his neighbour spreadeth a net for his feet. 6 In the transgression of an evil man there is a snare: but the righteous doth sing and rejoice. 7 The righteous considereth the cause of the poor: but the wicked regardeth not to know it. 8 Scornful men bring a city into a snare: but wise men turn away wrath. 9 If a wise man contendeth with a foolish man, whether he rage or laugh, there is no rest. 10 The bloodthirsty hate the upright: but the just seek his soul. 11 A fool uttereth all his mind: but a wise man keepeth it in till afterwards. 12 If a ruler hearken to lies, all his servants are wicked.

1 If you get more stubborn every time you are corrected, one day you will be crushed and never recover. 2 Show me a righteous ruler and I will show you a happy people. Show me a wicked ruler and I will show you a miserable people. 3 If you appreciate wisdom, your parents will be proud of you. It is a foolish waste to spend money on prostitutes. 4 When the king is concerned with justice, the nation will be strong, but when he is only concerned with money, he will ruin his country. 5 If you flatter your friends, you set a trap for yourself. 6 Evil people are trapped in their own sins, while honest people are happy and free. 7 A good person knows the rights of the poor, but wicked people cannot understand such things. 8 People with no regard for others can throw whole cities into turmoil. Those who are wise keep things calm. 9 When a wise man argues with a foolish one, he meets anger and ridicule without relief. 10 Bloodthirsty people hate anyone who's honest, but righteous people will protect the life of such a person. 11 Foolish people express their anger openly, but sensible people are patient and hold it back. 12 If a ruler pays attention to false information, all his officials will be liars.

13 The poor and the deceitful man meet together: the Lord lighteneth both their eyes. 14 The king that faithfully judgeth the poor, his throne shall be established for ever. 15 The rod and reproof give wisdom: but a child left to himself bringeth his mother to shame. 16 When the wicked are multiplied, transgression increaseth: but the righteous shall see their fall. 17 Correct thy son, and he shall give thee rest; yea, he shall give delight unto thy soul. 18 Where there is no vision, the people perish: but he that keepeth the law, happy is he. 19 A servant will not be corrected by words: for though he understand he will not answer. 20 Seest thou a man that is hasty in his words? there is more hope of a fool than of him. 21 He that delicately bringeth up his servant from a child shall have him become his son at the length. 22 An angry man stirreth up strife, and a furious man aboundeth in transgression. 23 A man's pride shall bring him low: but honour shall uphold the humble in spirit. 24 Whoso is partner with a thief hateth his own soul: he heareth cursing, and bewrayeth it not.

13 A poor person and his oppressor have this in common— the Lord gave eyes to both of them. 14 If a king defends the rights of the poor, he will rule for a long time. 15 Correction and discipline are good for children. If they have their own way, they will make their mothers ashamed of them. 16 When evil people are in power, crime increases. But the righteous will live to see the downfall of such people. 17 Discipline your children and you can always be proud of them. They will never give you reason to be ashamed. 18 Without a prophetic vision, the people throw off all restraint; but he who keeps God's law is happy. 19 You cannot correct servants just by talking to them. They may understand you, but they will pay no attention. 20 There is more hope for a fool than for someone who speaks without thinking. 21 If you give your servants everything they want from childhood on, some day they will take over everything you own. 22 People with quick tempers cause a lot of quarreling and trouble. 23 Arrogance will bring your downfall, but if you are humble, you will be respected. 24 The accomplice of a thief hates himself; he hears himself put under oath but discloses nothing.

25 The fear of man bringeth a snare: but whoso putteth his trust in the Lord shall be safe. 26 Many seek the ruler's favour; but every man's judgment cometh from the Lord. 27 An unjust man is an abomination to the just: and he that is upright in the way is abomination to the wicked. (Proverbs 29:1-27)

25 It is dangerous to be concerned with what others think of you, but if you trust the Lord, you are safe. 26 Everybody wants the good will of the ruler, but only from the Lord can you get justice. 27 The righteous hate the wicked, and the wicked hate the righteous. (Proverbs 29:1-27)

Proverbs - Day 30

1 The words of Agur the son of Jakeh, even the prophecy: the man spake unto Ithiel, even unto Ithiel and Ucal, 2 Surely I am more brutish than any man, and have not the understanding of a man. 3 I neither learned wisdom, nor have the knowledge of the holy. 4 Who hath ascended up into heaven, or descended? who hath gathered the wind in his fists? who hath bound the waters in a garment? who hath established all the ends of the earth? what is his name, and what is his son's name, if thou canst tell? 5 Every word of God is pure: he is a shield unto them that put their trust in him. 6 Add thou not unto his words, lest he reprove thee, and thou be found a liar. 7 Two things have I required of thee; deny me them not before I die: 8 Remove far from me vanity and lies: give me neither poverty nor riches; feed me with food convenient for me: 9 Lest I be full, and deny thee, and say, Who is the Lord? or lest I be poor, and steal, and take the name of my God in vain. 10 Accuse not a servant unto his master, lest he curse thee, and thou be found guilty. 11 There is a generation that curseth their father, and doth not bless their mother.

1 These are the solemn words of Agur son of Jakeh: 2 I am more boorish than anyone, I lack human discernment; 3 I have never learned any wisdom, and I know nothing at all about God. 4 Who has gone up to heaven and come down? Who has cupped the wind in the palms of his hands? Who has wrapped up the waters in his cloak? Who established all the ends of the earth? What is his name, and what is his son's name? Surely you know! 5 Every word of God's is pure; he shields those taking refuge in him. 6 If you claim that he said something that he never said, he will reprimand you and show that you are a liar." 7 I ask you, God, to let me have two things before I die: 8 keep me from lying, and let me be neither rich nor poor. So give me only as much food as I need. 9 If I have more, I might say that I do not need you. But if I am poor, I might steal and bring disgrace on my God. 10 Never criticize servants to their master. You will be cursed and suffer for it. 11 There are people who curse their fathers and do not show their appreciation for their mothers.

12 There is a generation that are pure in their own eyes, and yet is not washed from their filthiness. 13 There is a generation, O how lofty are their eyes! and their eyelids are lifted up. 14 There is a generation, whose teeth are as swords, and their jaw teeth as knives, to devour the poor from off the earth, and the needy from among men. 15 The horseleach hath two daughters, crying, Give, give. There are three things that are never satisfied, yea, four things say not, It is enough: 16 The grave; and the barren womb; the earth that is not filled with water; and the fire that saith not, It is enough. 17 The eye that mocketh at his father, and despiseth to obey his mother, the ravens of the valley shall pick it out, and the young eagles shall eat it. 18 There be three things which are too wonderful for me, yea, four which I know not: 19 The way of an eagle in the air; the way of a serpent upon a rock; the way of a ship in the midst of the sea; and the way of a man with a maid. 20 Such is the way of an adulterous woman; she eateth, and wipeth her mouth, and saith, I have done no wickedness. 21 For three things the earth is disquieted, and for four which it cannot bear: 22 For a servant when he reigneth; and a fool when he is filled with meat;

12 There are people who think they are pure when they are as filthy as they can be. 13 There are people who think they are so good—oh, how good they think they are! 14 There are people who take cruel advantage of the poor and needy; that is the way they make their living. 15 A leech has two daughters, and both are named "Give me!" There are four things that are never satisfied: 16 the world of the dead, a woman without children, dry ground that needs rain, and a fire burning out of control. 17 If you make fun of your father or despise your mother in her old age, you ought to be eaten by vultures or have your eyes picked out by wild ravens. 18 There are four things that are too mysterious for me to understand: 19 an eagle flying in the sky, a snake moving on a rock, a ship finding its way over the sea, and a man and a woman falling in love.
20 This is how an unfaithful wife acts: she commits adultery, takes a bath, and says, "But I haven't done anything wrong!" 21 There are four things that the earth itself cannot tolerate: 22 a slave who becomes a king, a fool who has all he wants to eat,

23 For an odious woman when she is married; and an handmaid that is heir to her mistress. 24 There be four things which are little upon the earth, but they are exceeding wise: 25 The ants are a people not strong, yet they prepare their meat in the summer; 26 The conies are but a feeble folk, yet make they their houses in the rocks; 27 The locusts have no king, yet go they forth all of them by bands; 28 The spider taketh hold with her hands, and is in kings' palaces. 29 There be three things which go well, yea, four are comely in going: 30 A lion which is strongest among beasts, and turneth not away for any; 31 A greyhound; an he goat also; and a king, against whom there is no rising up. 32 If thou hast done foolishly in lifting up thyself, or if thou hast thought evil, lay thine hand upon thy mouth. 33 Surely the churning of milk bringeth forth butter, and the wringing of the nose bringeth forth blood: so the forcing of wrath bringeth forth strife. (Proverbs 30:1-33)

23 a hateful woman who gets married, and a servant woman who takes the place of her mistress. 24 There are four animals in the world that are small, but very, very clever: 25 Ants: they are weak, but they store up their food in the summer. 26 Rock badgers: they are not strong either, but they make their homes among the rocks. 27 Locusts: they have no king, but they move in formation. 28 and the spiders, which you can catch in your hand, yet they are in the king's palace 29 There are four things that are impressive to watch as they walk: 30 lions, strongest of all animals and afraid of none; 31 the greyhound, the billy-goat and the king when his army is with him 32 If you have been foolish enough to be arrogant and plan evil, stop and think! 33 If you churn milk, you get butter. If you hit someone's nose, it bleeds. If you stir up anger, you get into trouble. (Proverbs 30:1-33)

Proverbs - Day 31

1 The words of king Lemuel, the prophecy that his mother taught him. 2 What, my son? and what, the son of my womb? and what, the son of my vows? 3 Give not thy strength unto women, nor thy ways to that which destroyeth kings. 4 It is not for kings, O Lemuel, it is not for kings to drink wine; nor for princes strong drink: 5 Lest they drink, and forget the law, and pervert the judgment of any of the afflicted. 6 Give strong drink unto him that is ready to perish, and wine unto those that be of heavy hearts. 7 Let him drink, and forget his poverty, and remember his misery no more. 8 Open thy mouth for the dumb in the cause of all such as are appointed to destruction. 9 Open thy mouth, judge righteously, and plead the cause of the poor and needy. 10 Who can find a virtuous woman? for her price is far above rubies. 11 The heart of her husband doth safely trust in her, so that he shall have no need of spoil. 12 She will do him good and not evil all the days of her life. 13 She seeketh wool, and flax, and worketh willingly with her hands. 14 She is like the merchants' ships; she bringeth her food from afar.

1 These are the solemn words which King Lemuel's mother said to him: 2 "You are my own dear son, the answer to my prayers. What shall I tell you? 3 Don't spend all your energy and all your money on women; they have destroyed kings. 4 Listen, Lemuel. Kings should not drink wine or have a craving for alcohol. 5 When they drink, they forget the laws and ignore the rights of people in need. 6 Alcohol is for people who are dying, for those who are in misery. 7 Let them drink and forget their poverty and unhappiness. 8 "Speak up for people who cannot speak for themselves. Protect the rights of all who are helpless. 9 Speak for them and be a righteous judge. Protect the rights of the poor and needy." 10 How hard it is to find a capable wife! She is worth far more than jewels! 11 Her husband puts his confidence in her, and he will never be poor. 12 As long as she lives, she does him good and never harm. 13 She keeps herself busy making wool and linen cloth. 14 She brings home food from out-of-the-way places, as merchant ships do.

15 She riseth also while it is yet night, and giveth meat to her household, and a portion to her maidens. 16 She considereth a field, and buyeth it: with the fruit of her hands she planteth a vineyard. 17 She girdeth her loins with strength, and strengtheneth her arms. 18 She perceiveth that her merchandise is good: her candle goeth not out by night. 19 She layeth her hands to the spindle, and her hands hold the distaff. 20 She stretcheth out her hand to the poor; yea, she reacheth forth her hands to the needy. 21 She is not afraid of the snow for her household: for all her household are clothed with scarlet. 22 She maketh herself coverings of tapestry; her clothing is silk and purple. 23 Her husband is known in the gates, when he sitteth among the elders of the land. 24 She maketh fine linen, and selleth it; and delivereth girdles unto the merchant. 25 Strength and honour are her clothing; and she shall rejoice in time to come. 26 She openeth her mouth with wisdom; and in her tongue is the law of kindness. 27 She looketh well to the ways of her household, and eateth not the bread of idleness. 28 Her children arise up, and call her blessed; her husband also, and he praiseth her.

15 She gets up before daylight to prepare food for her family and to tell her servant women what to do. 16 She looks at land and buys it, and with money she has earned she plants a vineyard. 17 She is a hard worker, strong and industrious. 18 She knows the value of everything she makes, and works late into the night. 19 She spins her own thread and weaves her own cloth. 20 She is generous to the poor and needy. 21 She doesn't worry when it snows, because her family has warm clothing. 22 She makes bedspreads and wears clothes of fine purple linen. 23 Her husband is well known, one of the leading citizens. 24 She makes clothes and belts, and sells them to merchants. 25 She is strong and respected and not afraid of the future. 26 She speaks with a gentle wisdom. 27 She is always busy and looks after her family's needs. 28 Her children show their appreciation, and her husband praises her.

29 Many daughters have done virtuously, but thou excellest them all. 30 Favour is deceitful, and beauty is vain: but a woman that feareth the Lord, she shall be praised. 31 Give her of the fruit of her hands; and let her own works praise her in the gates. (Proverbs 31:1-31)

29 He says, "Many women are good wives, but you are the best of them all." 30 Charm is deceptive and beauty disappears, but a woman who honors the Lord should be praised. 31 Give her credit for all she does. She deserves the respect of everyone. (Proverbs 31:1-31)

What do you think? Wasn't reading the book of Proverbs great! You took your time and read it through in just 31 days (1 Month)!

In so doing, you have undoubtedly become much wiser than you were just 31 days ago. While reading through the book of Proverbs, you should have noticed that specific topics or themes were often repeated. Repetition in the Bible indicates a point of emphasis; these are things that God would like to impress more deeply in your mind for your benefit. God understands how you learn and is cooperating with you in the learning process.

Learning is cumulative. For your part, you must re-read what you have already read repeatedly for the teaching to become deeply ingrained. You will achieve more significant results by learning in this method. Remember, Bible-influenced thoughts will produce better feelings, resulting in better actions and outcomes in your life.

> **Then said Jesus to those Jews which believed on him,** If ye continue in my word, **then are ye my disciples indeed; (John 8:31)**

The two most practical ways to please God during the day of your youth are (1) **Prayer** and (2) **reading the Bible, the Word of God**! Jesus declares His Word to be both spirit and life. This is so because Jesus' words are the words of God. When young people like yourself read and meditate on the Bible, you effectively build your life's foundation on the bedrock of the WORD of God. As a true disciple of Jesus Christ, you must be an avid reader and doer of the WORD of God. We will return to the practice of reading the WORD of God, the Bible, and provide you with more of a reading plan to help you make reading the WORD of God the Bible your favorite daily habit. But before we do that, let's discuss establishing a vibrant prayer life.

No doubt you all have heard the term "prayer life." The term "prayer life" is meant to convey that prayer is much more than saying grace over a meal or a few minutes of prayer at bedtime, but prayer life indicates that prayer is a way of life or a lifelong relationship with God. It is a daily and consistently active fellowship and communion with God. Communion means an instance of sharing thoughts or feelings or communication between those who are in a relationship.

The most fundamental part of our human and social existence lies in our ability to communicate with one another and build relationships. Life would be brutal and cold if no one could communicate with one another. Without communication, we could never establish relationships, and consequently, we would most likely self-destruct due to a lack of understanding of each other. Communication is critical to survival.

Communication, or the ability to relate, is compelling as it allows us to understand each other and work together. The Bible says the builders of the Tower of Babel were unlimited in what they could accomplish because of their ability to communicate and work together.

> **And the Lord said, Behold, the people is one, and they have all one language; and this they begin to do: and now nothing will be restrained from them, which they have imagined to do. (Genesis 11:6)**

The most incredible privilege of your life is establishing and maintaining a relationship with God Almighty and working with Him. You and God will accomplish great things in your life. God's perfect will, purpose, and plan for your life are waiting to be fulfilled. Your prayer life is the determining factor.

If you feel you lack this vital part of living for and pleasing God, you will be happy to know that the rest of this book is dedicated to helping you establish and maintain a vibrant and effective relationship with God through prayer.

Prayer in the Days of Your Youth

You, young person, know more about prayer than you give yourself credit for. Not me, you may say. But if we replaced the word prayer with the word communication, you would agree that you know how to communicate. Communication is something you do every day and all day. You have been communicating since the day you were born! Your first communication, the day of your birth, was a loud cry that informed those present that you were alive and needed some attention right away. Your parents were more than happy to respond to that communication and give you a warm embrace. Your first words were barely understandable as you learned to say mom-ma and dad-da. However, your communication continually improved as you began recognizing people and objects by name. You learned to combine words and form complete sentences as your vocabulary increased. Thus, you have been communicating your entire life. Prayer is a form of communication that is directed exclusively to God.

In learning to communicate, you learned there were specific protocols or rules to follow if you communicated well. First, you learned never to tell a lie and that you must always be honest. You learned to communicate kindness by saying "please and thank you." You learned to communicate respect by saying, "Yes sir, no sir, and yes ma'am, no ma'am." You learned which words in your vocabulary were acceptable and which were forbidden to use. These protocols allowed you to communicate appropriately.

As a young person, you have acquired the etiquette, knowledge of grammar, and skills required to communicate well. Therefore, you have a foundation to build a practical prayer life. So, how do you apply what you know about communicating to the idea of communicating with Almighty God? That is the question that this section of the book is dedicated to answering.

First, understand that prayer is communication and something you already know and are skilled at doing. You are not starting from scratch! You know how to communicate with your parents, friends, family, etc. You will now learn to adapt your communication skills to communicate spiritually with God. **"You are only as strong as your prayer life"** is a quote Sis. Ann Jackson often spoke to our youth to convey a truth and an urgency.

The truth is that your strength and stability in living for God depends on the strength of your relationship with God, which is your prayer life. The urgency is that you risk suffering a significant spiritual loss if your relationship with God, which is your prayer life, is not firmly established and maintained. You must establish your relationship with God, your prayer life, as soon as possible so that you become strong in the Lord and in the power of His might. There is no better time to establish a prayer life than now in your youth!

The days of your youth afford you a unique opportunity to spend quality time establishing a bona fide or genuine relationship (prayer life) with God. Later in life, you will have many responsibilities, competing for every minute of your precious time. Take full advantage of the free time your youth affords to establish this prayer life to the best of your ability. You will never regret having done so.

You already know how to communicate. Now, you will learn how to expand your communication skills to enter into and maintain a consistent daily spiritual relationship with God.

The words pray, prayer, prayers, prayest, prayeth, and praying occur over 465 times in the Word of God, the Bible. The Old Testament Hebrew root of these words, tefillah, means to entreat, to intercede, to make supplication.

Intreat - to ask (a person) earnestly; beg or plead with; implore. To make an earnest request or petition for (something)

Intercede - to intervene on behalf of another to influence what is happening or to prevent undesirable consequences.

Supplication - asking, appealing, or begging for something earnestly or humbly from someone who can grant a request.

The Greek root of the New Testament word prayer is proseuche, meaning to worship or supplicate.

Worship - to show respect by engaging in acts of prayer and devotion.

As you can see from the Old and New Testament definitions of prayer above, prayer is a different form of communication. The form of communication you use with peers is informal; with adults and seniors, it's formal, but with God, it is spiritual and worshipful. Therefore, you must learn new protocols to help you acclimate or adjust to communicating with God in a spiritual context or environment.

Protocols of Prayer

Just as there are rules or protocols for proper verbal communication, such as never telling a lie, always saying please and thank you, etc., there are protocols for appropriate and effective communication with God. Yes, prayer is communication, but it is toward Almighty God. Your attitude and vocabulary while communicating with others will vary depending on who the other individual is. For example, you communicate differently with friends your age than you communicate with adults and seniors. Right? When you do so, you follow a protocol whereby communication with your peers is informal and loose, and communication with adults and seniors is more formal and respectful.

Since God is an invisible spirit and cannot be seen with the human eye, communication with God through prayer becomes a spiritual undertaking. This spiritual aspect of prayer makes it different from the communication you are familiar with. Being spiritual, prayer becomes an element of your worship or devotion to God, which leads us to the first protocol for prayer: faith.

Prayer Protocol #1: Faith

The most fundamental element in the worship of God is faith or trust that God exists. It is called agnostic to hold the view that the reality of God is unknown or unknowable. Atheists are those who do not believe in the existence of God. The agnostics and the atheists both lack faith. The book of **Psalms 14:1** states, "The fool hath said in his heart, there is no God..." Only faith can enable you to believe and trust in what is unseen or invisible to your eyes. That is why the Scripture declares emphatically that without faith, it is impossible to please God. You must have faith. (See below)

But without faith it is impossible to please him: **for he that cometh to God must believe that he is**, and that he is a rewarder of them that diligently seek him. **(Hebrews 11:6)**

No one can please God without faith, for whoever comes to God must have faith that God exists and rewards those who seek him. **(Hebrews 11:6)**

How do you, young person, know that God exists? Answer: You go outside and behold all the natural marvels of the creation of heaven and earth, the beautiful sky, clouds, sun, moon, stars, trees, plants, animal life, and human life. In so doing, you should instantly recognize that only a higher power could have created all these things in such an intelligent, orderly, and wonderous way. If you further consider the heights of great mountains, the depths of the ocean, and the tremendous power of the forces of nature, you are left in profound awe of the Creator. Creation itself is considered, by scripture, to be undeniable and inexcusable evidence of the existence of God. (See **Romans 1:20** below).

> **For the invisible things of him from the creation of the world are clearly seen, being understood by the things that are made, even his eternal power and Godhead; so that they are without excuse: (Romans 1:20)**
>
> Ever since God created the world, his invisible qualities, both his eternal power and his divine nature, have been clearly seen; they are perceived in the things that God has made. So those people have no excuse at all! (Romans 1:20)

One of Jesus' disciples is called doubting Thomas, because he refused to believe Jesus rose from the dead without physical and visual evidence of Jesus' resurrection. Thankfully, Jesus did not take offense at Thomas's doubtful attitude but saw it as a teachable moment. Jesus made a special appearance to Thomas, allowing him to physically touch the nailed scarred hands and the spear-punctured side of His resurrected body. He urged Thomas never to doubt but to believe, saying how blessed they were who would believe without proof or physical evidence. That is what faith is: the evidence of things not seen. That is the faith you must have to establish a relationship, a prayer life, with God. You have never seen nor touched the resurrected body of Jesus Christ, yet you believe Jesus was crucified and was resurrected from the dead. You have faith.

> **Jesus saith unto him, Thomas, because thou hast seen me, thou hast believed: blessed are they that have not seen, and yet have believed. (John 20:29)**
>
> Jesus said to him, "Have you believed because you have seen me? How blessed are those who do not see me, but believe anyway! (John 20:29)

You, young person, are not an agnostic nor atheist because you have faith in God. You know God exists. You cannot see God, but you believe the evidence of the existence of God in the creation. You are no fool. Your faith will enable you to establish a relationship with God, a prayer life. Your faith will cause you to understand that God is an active participant on the other end of your prayer communication; God is listening, watching, and reacting to your prayer. As your relationship with God and your prayer life grows more intimate and powerful, you will experience an anointing of God in your prayer life that confirms or validates your faith.

According to **Hebrews 11:6**, you must believe in God in two ways. First, you believe that God exists, and second, you believe that God is a rewarder of those who diligently seek Him. You can have faith that God exists but simultaneously doubt that God will answer your prayer. The attitude and the language of your prayer must be faithful (pun intended) or full of faith so that you not only believe in the God to whom you pray but also believe God can respond to your requests according to His will. You must never pray to God with doubt. However, it is good to ask God, in your prayer, to help you overcome any unbelief.

Doubt or unbelief will defeat your prayer communication, as God will never respond favorably to unbelief. God rewards only faith. Imagine praying to God with these words, "God, I know that you will say no and never give me the answer I desire, but here is my request..." That is an extreme example of doubt, and you must avoid this in your spirit and attitude when communicating with God. You must believe that God exists and pray in faith. An example of a faithful prayer would be, "God, I thank you for I know that you hear and answer prayer; please let it be your will and good pleasure to grant that..."

| If any of you lack wisdom, let him ask of God, that giveth to all men liberally, and upbraideth not; and it shall be given him. 6 But let him ask in faith, nothing wavering. For he that wavereth is like a wave of the sea driven with the wind and tossed. 7 For let not that man think that he shall receive any thing of the Lord. (James 1:5-7) | But if any of you lack wisdom, you should pray to God, who will give it to you; because God gives generously and graciously to all. 6 But when you pray, you must believe and not doubt at all. Whoever doubts is like a wave in the sea that is driven and blown about by the wind. 7-8 If you are like that, unable to make up your mind and undecided in all you do, you must not think that you will receive anything from the Lord. (James 1:5-8) |

Young person, you must never pray to God without expecting an answer. You may not know when, where, or how God will answer, but you must believe God will answer according to His will and purpose. Your relationship with God will be as dynamic as any. God will answer your prayers dynamically. Sometimes God will answer "Yes," sometimes God will answer "No," and sometimes God will answer "Not right now." You must never try to prejudge or predetermine God's answer to your prayers. You believe and allow God to answer according to His will and purpose for your life. Only ensure your prayers are appropriate and worthy of the great God to whom you pray. This brings us to our second protocol of prayer: Sincerity.

Prayer Protocol #2: Sincerity

God has high expectations regarding your prayer life's genuineness, honesty, and purity. If you are not sincere in your communication with God, you are attempting to build a relationship with God based on dishonesty and falsehood, which will never work. The word sincere in the Bible comes from the Greek word eilikrines, which means to be judged by sunlight, tested as genuine or pure. Young person, God knows if you are sincere when attempting to communicate with Him. You must always be honest.

Sincerity before God in prayer is not just a reference to the words spoken but also to your demeanor, approach, and attitude in prayer. Your prayer communication with God must always be close or personal. God should always be the one and exclusive recipient of your prayer communication. Your prayer should never be an outward display to impress others around you. Neither should you ever assume a prayer posture such as kneeling with your head bowed and your eyes closed with no intention to communicate with God sincerely, but only give the appearance of praying. In doing this, you are building a bad habit of false or insincere prayer, which will become an established habit that will do you no good spiritually. You must ensure you are sincere and give God your very best effort to connect with Him in prayer each time you bow your knees and assume a prayer posture. God is not looking for perfection in your communication with Him. He's looking for sincerity. That is the singleness of your heart towards God. God has your time and attention in prayer. You must not be distracted when communicating with God.

Your established prayer life will be the heart of your faith walk with God and must be maintained pure and sincere, absent of any falsehood or pretense. Your sincerity ensures your prayer counts and is rewarded by God! God greatly desires a relationship with you, young person, but let it be one of sincerity.

> **Now therefore** fear the Lord, and serve him in sincerity and in truth: **(Joshua 24:14)**
>
> **Grace be with all them that love our Lord Jesus Christ** in sincerity. **Amen. (Ephesians 6:24)**

Prayer Protocol #3: Intimacy

In the scripture above, Jesus teaches how prayer should be performed or enacted. Prayer with God requires spiritual intimacy or closeness. To make his point, Jesus gives a mental image of entering a closet, referring to a small private chamber that lends itself to intimacy. He then says close the door, indicating a complete shut-in with God. As you pray, you accomplish this intimacy internally within your mind, spirit, or inner man. It is a mental/spiritual shut-in with God and can be achieved in a private prayer setting when you are alone or in a public prayer setting, such as a pre-service prayer where others are present. It involves a mental/spiritual focus on God. You cannot achieve spiritual intimacy in your prayer to God if you are looking around, distracted, or mentally and spiritually disengaged from God. Bringing your mental and spiritual focus into that secret or intimate place with God takes much effort, but it is well worth it. Again, you can achieve intimacy in your prayer to God in private or public settings. If your prayer with God never reaches that intimacy, whether in private or public, you have not connected with God in the way God expects. Have you ever had a conversation with someone who was distracted? They could barely keep up with the details of your discussion and constantly looked away from you to observe other happenings. That scenario has no intimacy, as the other person is disengaged and distracted. That is not an enjoyable experience. You want the person you're communicating with to pay attention and respond to what you are saying. Right?

In an intimate conversation, the person you are communicating with will look you in the eye directly, indicate understanding with gestures like nodding of the head, and follow the details of what you share, because they are interested and engaged in what you have to say. Your relationship with God, your prayer life, must be carried out or performed with intimacy. When you pray, do your best to stay focused and engaged as you enter the secret place of the Most High.

> And when thou prayest, thou shalt not be as the hypocrites are: for they love to pray standing in the synagogues and in the corners of the streets, that they may be seen of men. Verily I say unto you, They have their reward. 6 But thou, **when thou prayest, enter into thy closet**, and when thou hast **shut thy door, pray to thy Father which is in secret**; and thy Father which seeth in secret shall reward thee openly. 7 But when ye pray, **use not vain repetitions**, as the heathen do: for they think that they shall be heard for their much speaking. 8 Be not ye therefore like unto them: for your Father knoweth what things ye have need of, before ye ask him.that diligently seek him. ([Matthew 6:5-8](#))
>
> When you pray, do not be like the hypocrites! They love to stand up and pray in the houses of worship and on the street corners, so that everyone will see them. I assure you, they have already been paid in full. 6 But **when you pray, go to your room, close the door, and pray to your Father, who is unseen**. And your Father, who sees what you do in private, will reward you. 7 "When you pray, **do not use a lot of meaningless words**, as the pagans do, who think that their gods will hear them because their prayers are long. 8 Do not be like them. Your Father already knows what you need before you ask him.. ([Matthew 6:5-8](#))

Prayer Protocol #4: Imagination

Everyone has an imagination. It was given to us by God. Yet, too often, our imaginations are misused for the gratification of our carnal nature. Prayer is an opportunity to use your imagination as God intended. Therefore, you must learn to involve your imagination in prayer for the most significant benefit. Your faith is your spiritual eyesight; it enables you to believe the evidence of things not seen. Your imagination creates mental images of things or happenings not present to your senses. In this way, your imagination allows you to connect better or understand. For example, the God you are establishing a relationship with is unseen.

Still, you can use your imagination to visualize yourself kneeling and bowing at God's throne while praying. This mental image of God on His throne actively listening to your prayer will affect it, making it more realistic and practical. That is the most significant use of your imagination. So, if you are offering thanks to God for His love towards you, you will visualize Jesus Christ giving His life for you on the cross. If you are offering thanks to God for your born-again experience, you envision Christ Jesus alive and raised from the dead with power, etc. This is where the habit of Bible reading helps greatly. Bible reading gives you ample spiritual thoughts for which mental images can be created in their context and used in prayer.

Your faith, sincerity, intimacy, and imagination will all work together to help you pray fervent and effectual prayers that eventually avail. This is what you want; therefore, this is what you must practice.

Elements of Prayer

Now that you understand the basic rules or protocols for effective and appropriate communication with God (faith, sincerity, intimacy, and imagination), let's discuss the specifics of prayer and its forms. Prayer can be silent (said in your heart) or audible (spoken out loud). Sometimes, it is more appropriate to pray silently, such as when you are at school or work and do not want to draw attention to yourself. Then, you can pray silently. Otherwise, it is appropriate and expected of you to use your voice to pray audibly. The most significant use of your voice is in communication with God. Pre-service prayer is an example of an appropriate time to pray audibly as it is designated for collective prayer as a Body of Christ and for creating a worshipful atmosphere with blended voices of prayer.

You can communicate with God from different postures, such as kneeling, bowing, sitting, lying, standing, or walking, as long as you can maintain the protocols of prayer (**faith, sincerity, intimacy, and imagination**) while doing so. A kneeling and bowing prayer posture gives a greater sense of humility when you pray and should be preferred.

Prayer, because it is spiritual and is an element of worship and devotion, can and will be different from any other form of communication. For instance, it would be considered too dramatic in a regular conversation to repeat phrases or over-emphasize emotionally. But in a worshipful atmosphere of prayer, it is appropriate to express feelings of love and awe towards God emotionally and dramatically. It may be hard to do otherwise when your spirit and emotions are fully engaged and are touched by God's anointing as you yield to God in prayer. Your words may become unintelligible during prayer as the Spirit of God gives you a spiritual utterance. You gain much spiritual strength as you build up your most holy faith during these particular times of prayer. Young people can and should experience much power and anointing in their prayer life.

Outside of having the experience of being overwhelmed by God's spirit in prayer, your communication with God should be clear and understandable. It is inappropriate to use vain repetitions. That is to repeat words emptily with no mental or spiritual substance. Words that may have meaning but are meaningless in the context of your expressing them. For example, let's say you are praying during pre-service, and you notice that there are five minutes left in pre-service prayer, so you begin to ramble, speaking words only to fill up five minutes.

It would be best to avoid this, as that would qualify as vain repetition. You must ensure you communicate with God when you assume a prayer posture and begin praying. Otherwise, you are establishing a bad habit of false prayer.

If you have nothing else to say to God at that moment, remain in your prayer posture, remain spiritually engaged, and take a few minutes to listen in your spirit or inner man for God to speak back to you. Prayer is a relationship between two, you and God. You are not listening necessarily for an audible voice of God but an impression (a still, small voice) that God can make on your spirit regarding the things you have prayed to God about. In so doing, you may have something else to say to God in response.

Jesus gave His disciples a template or model for prayer. They were not to repeat the words of His model prayer verbatim but were to ensure they understood and used the specific elements found in His model prayer in their prayer. Jesus said to His disciples, "After this manner, therefore pray ye." So, young person, here is how you should pray.

Prayer Element #1 – Reverence and Awe

"**Our Father which art in heaven.**" Jesus taught you to begin your prayer by acknowledging that you are communicating with your Father in Heaven! You are not, in prayer, communicating with your peer, equal, or even with another human. You are endeavoring to communicate with Almighty God, the creator of Heaven and earth. Your conscious acknowledgment of God at the beginning of your prayer should invoke the necessary attitude of profound reverence and awe. There must be in you some of what the prophet Isaiah felt when he, in a vision, saw God sitting on His throne. **Isaiah 6:5**: "Then said I, Woe is me! for I am undone; because I am a man of unclean lips, and I dwell in the midst of a people of unclean lips: for mine eyes have seen the King, the Lord of hosts." Isaiah was fear-struck, having seen the glory of God. You should also be in awe and reverence; but your fear of God is tempered by the fact that you also acknowledge God as your Father, "a term of endearment". Young person, let there be a deep reverence and awe in your heart for Almighty God.

Here is a sample of the reactions of those who encountered God: Gideon cried, Alas, O lord God! (**Judges 6:22**); Manoah, Sampson's father, thought he would die (**Judge 13:22**); Job said, "I abhor myself and repent in dust and ashes (**Job 42:6**); Daniel said, "There is no more strength in me; for my comeliness is turned in me to corruption (**Daniel 10:8**); Simon Peter said, "Depart from me; for I am a sinful man, O Lord (**Luke 5:8**); John fell at His feet as dead (**Revelations 1:17**). All of these were in awe of God.

Your expression of reverence and awe toward God can be phrased however you wish, "Eternal God, Eternal Savior, Father, Heavenly Father, Lord Jesus, My Lord, My God, My King, My Savior, etc." However, as a general rule, you should begin your prayer with an expression of reverence and awe, as it helps set an appropriate tone within you for communicating with God. This will ensure your communication with God is never trivial or trite. You are communicating with Almighty God, who's in a much higher position than you.

Be not rash with thy mouth, and let not thine heart be hasty to utter any thing before God: for God is in heaven, and thou upon earth: therefore let thy words be few. (**Ecclesiastes 5:2**)

But our God is in the heavens: he hath done whatsoever he hath pleased. (**Psalms 115:3**)

Let us lift up our heart with our hands unto God in the heavens. (**Lamentations 3:41**)

Prayer Element #2 – Worship and Praise

"**Hallowed be thy name.**" The Greek word for hallowed is hagiazo, which means venerate or honor. Jesus taught there is to be an element of worship towards the name of God in our communication with God. Many scripture references demonstrate the worship of God's name. (see below)

> And let thy name be magnified for ever, saying, The Lord of hosts is the God over Israel: and let the house of thy servant David be established before thee. (2 Samuel 7:26)
>
> Then the Levites, Jeshua, and Kadmiel, Bani, Hashabniah, Sherebiah, Hodijah, Shebaniah, and Pethahiah, said, Stand up and bless the Lord your God for ever and ever: and blessed be thy glorious name, which is exalted above all blessing and praise. (Nehemiah 9:5)
>
> He sent redemption unto his people: he hath commanded his covenant for ever: holy and reverend is his name. (Psalms 111:9)
>
> For from the rising of the sun even unto the going down of the same my name shall be great among the Gentiles; and in every place incense shall be offered unto my name, and a pure offering: for my name shall be great among the heathen, saith the Lord of hosts. (Malachi 1:11)
>
> Now therefore, our God, we thank thee, and praise thy glorious name. (1 Chronicles 29:13)
>
> And blessed be his glorious name for ever: and let the whole earth be filled with his glory; Amen, and Amen. (Psalms 72:19)
>
> Not unto us, O Lord, not unto us, but unto thy name give glory, for thy mercy, and for thy truth's sake. (Psalms 115:1)
>
> Father, glorify thy name. Then came there a voice from heaven, saying, I have both glorified it, and will glorify it again. (John 12:28)

Phrase this element in a manner of your choosing, young person, but your communication with God must include an aspect of worship and praise toward the name of God, Jesus.

God's people, the Jews or Israelites, held God's name in such high regard that they refused to even speak His name for fear that they would speak His name in vain. Jesus, the revealed name of God, is the name we worship. Jesus' name is the name that is above all names. Jesus' name means God saves or God (Jehovah) has become our savior. In the name of Jesus, every knee shall bow, and every tongue shall confess. You, young person, must establish your relationship with God and your prayer life with worship and praise to the wonderful name of Jesus.

> By him therefore let us offer the sacrifice of praise to God continually, that is, **the fruit of our lips giving thanks to his name.** (**Hebrews 13:15**)
>
> Therefore will I give thanks unto thee, O Lord, among the heathen, **and sing praises unto thy name.** (**Psalms 18:49**)

Prayer Element #3 – Submission and Surrender

"**Thy Kingdom come, Thy will be done.**" The word Kingdom speaks to the royalty of God as King and the realm over which God rules and reigns. Jesus is teaching that our prayer should include a longing in our hearts for God's Kingdom and rule to come, as we know that God's Kingdom and rule would be the best thing that could ever happen in our lives. God is holy, just, righteous, merciful, kind and loving. Let His Kingdom come! Young person, when you pray, let your kingdom come. You are expressing a desire for a better life.

That is the essence of this element of prayer. You desire to be a part of God's great Kingdom and rule, young person, so you submit yourself to God. Your submission is honest, as is God's rule or Kingship. You are willing to follow the direction and leading of God through His delegate, your pastor.

Express your feelings of submission to God in your prayer by phrasing in whatever manner you please. "God, I surrender, I belong to you, I yield myself to you, I'm bought with a price, etc."

Jesus, in the garden of Gethsemane (olive press), crushed his own human will in favor of the will of God, which was for Him to endure the cross and despise the shame so that you, young person, could be saved.

Submission is not the easiest thing to do, but it is necessary and, when done from the heart, will pay huge dividends in your life as you submit and become a true citizen of God's spiritual kingdom.

> And he went a little farther, and fell on his face, and prayed, saying, O my Father, if it be possible, let this cup pass from me: **nevertheless not as I will, but as thou wilt.** (**Matthew 26:39**)

> He went a little farther on, threw himself face downward on the ground, and prayed, "My Father, if it is possible, take this cup of suffering from me! **Yet not what I want, but what you want.** (**Matthew 26:39**)

As a true citizen of God's kingdom, young person, you live to do God's will and that which is well pleasing in the sight of God. When you make submission and surrender part of your prayer, you constantly remind God and yourself of your desire and commitment to "thy kingdom come, and thy will be done."

Forasmuch then as Christ hath suffered for us in the flesh, arm yourselves likewise with the same mind: for he that hath suffered in the flesh hath ceased from sin; 2 That he no longer should live the rest of his time in the flesh to the lusts of men, but to the will of God. (1 Peter 4:1-2)	**Since Christ suffered physically, you too must strengthen yourselves with the same way of thinking that he had; because whoever suffers physically is no longer involved with sin. 2 From now on, then, you must live the rest of your earthly lives controlled by God's will and not by human desires. (1 Peter 4:1-2)**

Prayer Element #4 – Supplication and Intercession

"**Give us this day our daily bread.**" Supplication is asking, appealing, or begging for something earnestly or humbly from someone who can grant a request. Jesus uses the word bread in His model prayer to encompass anything you need to survive. Intercession is intervening or supplicating on behalf of another to influence what is happening or prevent undesirable consequences.

In supplication to God, you acknowledge that you do not have the means to survive independently, but you know that your sustenance (nourishment and livelihood) and help come from the Lord. When the children of Israel were delivered from Egyptian bondage, they were given, by God, daily manna (bread). God also provided them with water and ensured their shoes never wore out. God wanted them to know that they could trust Him for their survival. You, young person, can trust God to do the same for you.

Phrase your request to God in any manner you choose. Only ensure your supplication is appropriate. Asking God to supply your needs is reasonable, but asking God to supply your wants is inappropriate. For example, you will need transportation to school, work, home, and church, and it is appropriate to ask God to supply your transportation needs. But asking God for a $2.3 million Aston Martin Vulcan car is inappropriate, as that is called asking amiss that you may consume it upon your lust.

God expects you, young person, to express your dependence and faith that only God can supply your needs. You express this dependence on God by prayer and supplication.

> **Be careful for nothing; but in every thing by prayer and supplication with thanksgiving let your requests be made known unto God. (Philippians 4:6)**
>
> **Praying always with all prayer and supplication in the Spirit, and watching thereunto with all perseverance and supplication for all saints; (Ephesians 6:18)**

In the same way that you supplicate for your own needs, you can and should supplicate on behalf of others' needs. This would be called intercessory prayer. When you pray an intercessory prayer, it is with the same earnestness and intensity as you would pray for yourself. Who knows if God would like to use you to intercede on behalf of a friend or family member? In a world that thinks of nothing but "me," "myself," and "I," you can make a huge difference by praying for others. As a youth, you have the time to pray when others cannot.

Prayer Element #5 – Repentance & Confession

"**Forgive us our debts.**" Repentance is what makes prayer so powerful and essential for you. Jesus is teaching you that prayer is a reasonable and appropriate time to repeatedly ask God for forgiveness of your sins, shortcomings, and failures. In so doing, you clear yourself or your conscience, and only then can you continue your relationship with God. Sin breaks your relationship with God. You may not realize the effect of sin on your relationship with God because the judgment of sin is not executed speedily. Nevertheless, you cannot maintain a relationship with God with unrepented sin in your life. You must never be deceived regarding sin. Whatever you sow, you will reap eventually. You do not want to reap the harvest of sin in your life. So, you repent often, even daily, in your prayers. Repentance is the mechanism of maintenance in your relationship with God once established. When repentance is a part of your communication to God, you continually remind yourself and God that you are flesh and blood, and as such, you're aware that you are subject to sin and failure. You don't want to sin, but if you fail and miss the mark, you want God to forgive and help you immediately. Praying this way also lessens your tolerance for sin because, in doing so, you search your heart daily before God.

Confession is acknowledging and admitting your sin to God in detail as remorsefully as possible. Repentance is to turn away from sin and not participate in it.

Again, you should phrase your repentance and confession how you please but repent sincerely from the depths of your soul. There are plenty of Bible references for how to repent and confess. For example, **Psalms 51** below is general repentance, but **Nehemiah 9** below is the confession of specific sins.

> **Have mercy upon me, O God, according to thy lovingkindness: according unto the multitude of thy tender mercies blot out my transgressions. 2 Wash me throughly from mine iniquity, and cleanse me from my sin. 3 For I acknowledge my transgressions: and my sin is ever before me. 4 Against thee, thee only, have I sinned, and done this evil in thy sight:** that thou mightest be justified when thou speakest, and be clear when thou judgest. 5 Behold, I was shapen in iniquity; and in sin did my mother conceive me. 6 Behold, thou desirest truth in the inward parts: and in the hidden part thou shalt make me to know wisdom. 7 Purge me with hyssop, and I shall be clean: wash me, and I shall be whiter than snow. 8 Make me to hear joy and gladness; that the bones which thou hast broken may rejoice. 9 Hide thy face from my sins, and blot out all mine iniquities. 10 Create in me a clean heart, O God; and renew a right spirit within me. 11 Cast me not away from thy presence; and take not thy holy spirit from me. (**Psalms 51:1-11**)
>
> 16 But they and our fathers dealt proudly, and hardened their necks, and hearkened not to thy commandments, 17 And refused to obey, neither were mindful of thy wonders that thou didst among them; but hardened their necks, and in their rebellion **appointed a captain to return to their bondage**: but thou art a God ready to pardon, gracious and merciful, slow to anger, and of great kindness, and forsookest them not. 18 Yea, **when they had made them a molten calf**, and said, **This is thy God that brought thee up out of Egypt**, and had wrought great provocations; (**Nehemiah 9:16-18**)

Please, understand young person that you cannot worship or praise God through unrepented sin. That is a bad habit to develop. That will cause you to lose your sincerity before God. God is listening only to a sincere prayer.

18 If I regard iniquity in my heart, the Lord will not hear me: (**Psalms 66:18**)	18 If I had ignored my sins, the Lord would not have listened to me. (**Psalms 66:18**)

Prayer Element #6 – Forgiveness

"<u>**As we forgive our debtors**</u>." It should mean the world to you, young person, that God mercifully grants forgiveness for your sins, shortcomings, and weaknesses and allows you to continue in your relationship with Himself. You should be greatly humbled beyond words for such mercy, love, and kindness as shown by God.

And as a recipient of God's forgiveness and undeserved favor, God expects you to do likewise and forgive others who have wronged you. It is very offensive to God when you harbor unforgiveness in your heart toward others while receiving God's forgiveness for yourself. In this scenario, God suspends forgiveness. Jesus says to be reconciled with your brother before you even bring an offering to God, or you risk God not accepting your sacrifice. Forgiveness, being a part of your prayer, ensures you've searched your heart for any offenses incurred from others, that those offenses are truly forgiven, and that you are treating others the same as God has treated you, with mercy and forgiveness. This element of prayer has more to do with your actions and attitude than with your words. You, young person, are to emulate God by forgiving others as God has forgiven you.

> **For if ye forgive men their trespasses, your heavenly Father will also forgive you: 15 But if ye forgive not men their trespasses, neither will your Father forgive your trespasses. (Matthew 6:14-15)**
>
> **Then came Peter to him, and said, Lord, how oft shall my brother sin against me, and I forgive him? till seven times? 22 Jesus saith unto him, I say not unto thee, Until seven times: but, Until seventy times seven. (Matthew 18:21-**

FORGIVENESS

Prayer Element #7 – Leniency & Deliverance

"**And lead us not into temptation.**" The word temptation here means to put to proof or to test. In praying that God does not put you to the test, you admit that you have no confidence in yourself and understand that you are but flesh and blood. You also acknowledge that God will test your sincerity, so you ask for leniency as you do not desire hard testing for fear of failing God.

> 41 Watch and pray, that ye enter not into temptation: the spirit indeed is willing, but the flesh is weak. (**Matthew 26:41**)

This makes sense to you, right? As a young person, having a grounded view of yourself keeps you humble before God. In this way, God can help you. Many young people make the mistake of feeling invincible; consequently, pride creeps in and ruins their humility before God.

"**but deliver us from evil.**" Deliverance from evil means to be rescued from the influence of the enemy, the devil, and all that is hurtful, harmful, bad, wicked, lewd, grievous, etc. In praying for deliverance from evil, you declare your allegiance to the side of good. You make it plain that you would have nothing to do with evil as you know the result of allowing such influence of evil in your life. You even ask God to destroy the enemy and these influences that attempt to derail your faith and walk with God. This is a serious part of prayer, as there is some spiritual warfare in praying for deliverance from evil. Young people must fight the good warfare against sin, their flesh, and the devil. You accomplish this by fasting and praying that God delivers you from evil.

| 13 There hath no temptation taken you but such as is common to man: but God is faithful, who will not suffer you to be tempted above that ye are able; but will with the temptation also make a way to escape, that ye may be able to bear it. (**1 Corinthians 10:13**) | 13 Every test that you have experienced is the kind that normally comes to people. But God keeps his promise, and he will not allow you to be tested beyond your power to remain firm; at the time you are put to the test, he will give you the strength to endure it, and so provide you with a way out. (**1 Corinthians 10:13**) |

10 And Jabez called on the God of Israel, saying, Oh that thou wouldest bless me indeed, and enlarge my coast, and that thine hand might be with me, and that thou wouldest keep me from evil, that it may not grieve me! And God granted him that which he requested. (**1 Chronicles 4:10**)

10 But Jabez prayed to the God of Israel, "Bless me, God, and give me much land. Be with me and keep me from anything evil that might cause me pain." And God gave him what he prayed for. (**1 Chronicles 4:10**)

"For thine is the kingdom and the power and the glory forever, amen."

Jesus closes his model prayer the same way he opened it with more praise and adoration to the sovereign and eternal God.

Young person this is how you establish and maintain a vibrant and effective relationship with God!

Sure, we've discussed a lot but you do not have to memorize nor speak the words of Jesus' model prayer verbatim or exactly as Jesus said it. It is a model prayer, a template for you to follow.

Still, you should personalize and incorporate these **protocols** and **elements** into your prayer relationship with God.

Start talking to God in your way today, but remember what you have learned. Your approach to communicating with God will make all the difference in your relationship. The greatest relationship in your life's journey will be your relationship with God, which is your prayer life.

God is not looking for the beauty of your prayer or the pretty words. God is not looking for the arithmetic of your prayers or the number of words you use. God is looking for the sincerity of your prayer and how honest and faithful you are when you bow your knees in prayer.

Protocols of Prayer	Elements of Prayer
Faith	Reverence and Awe
Sincerity	Worship and Praise
Intimacy	Submission and Surrender
Imagination	Supplication and Intercession
	Repentance and Confession
	Forgiveness
	Leniency and Deliverance

Twenty (20) Days of Prayer

You are now ready to establish a genuine prayer life with God. To help you, we have selected Biblical prayers and list them in two versions of the Bible.

Study the selected prayers on the following pages with great interest and desire, seeking to know how the recorded prayers of the Bible were spoken. In so doing, you will, in these next 20 days, absorb some of the spirit of these prayers.

The Bible is your prayer textbook. Over time, with much Bible reading and praying, you will find yourself praying the Bible as you will feel the same sentiments as those you read about in the Bible. Biblical prayers will easily become the sentiment of your heart as well. This is another benefit of reading the Bible.

For the next 20 consecutive days, read the following pages Read only one prayer page daily, but feel free to re-read each day's prayers as many times as you wish.

Genuine prayer and Bible study are the most practical ways to please God in your youth. You are on your way to seizing every opportunity God has given you to excel and enjoy a purposeful and fulfilling life in God.

Prayer - Day 1

A prayer of David

1 Hear the right, O Lord, attend unto my cry, give ear unto my prayer, that goeth not out of feigned lips. 2 Let my sentence come forth from thy presence; let thine eyes behold the things that are equal. 3 Thou hast proved mine heart; thou hast visited me in the night; thou hast tried me, and shalt find nothing; I am purposed that my mouth shall not transgress. 4 Concerning the works of men, by the word of thy lips I have kept me from the paths of the destroyer. 5 Hold up my goings in thy paths, that my footsteps slip not. 6 I have called upon thee, for thou wilt hear me, O God: incline thine ear unto me, and hear my speech. 7 Shew thy marvellous lovingkindness, O thou that savest by thy right hand them which put their trust in thee from those that rise up against them. 8 Keep me as the apple of the eye, hide me under the shadow of thy wings, 9 From the wicked that oppress me, from my deadly enemies, who compass me about. 10 They are inclosed in their own fat: with their mouth they speak proudly. 11 They have now compassed us in our steps: they have set their eyes bowing down to the earth; 12 Like as a lion that is greedy of his prey, and as it were a young lion lurking in secret places. 13 Arise, O Lord, disappoint him, cast him down: deliver my soul from the wicked, which is thy sword:

1 Listen, O Lord, to my plea for justice; pay attention to my cry for help! Listen to my honest prayer. 2 You will judge in my favor, because you know what is right. 3 You know my heart. You have come to me at night; you have examined me completely and found no evil desire in me. I speak no evil, 14 as others do; I have obeyed your command and have not followed paths of violence. 5 my steps hold steadily to your paths, my feet do not slip. 6 I pray to you, O God, because you answer me; so turn to me and listen to my words. 7 Reveal your wonderful love and save me; at your side I am safe from my enemies. 8 Protect me as you would your very eyes; hide me in the shadow of your wings 9 from the attacks of the wicked. Deadly enemies surround me; 10 they close their hearts to compassion; they speak arrogantly with their mouths. 11 They are around me now, wherever I turn, watching for a chance to pull me down. 12 They are like lions, waiting for me, wanting to tear me to pieces.13 Come, Lord! Oppose my enemies and defeat them! Save me from the wicked by your sword;

14 From men which are thy hand, O Lord, from men of the world, which have their portion in this life, and whose belly thou fillest with thy hid treasure: they are full of children, and leave the rest of their substance to their babes. 15 As for me, I will behold thy face in righteousness: I shall be satisfied, when I awake, with thy likeness. (Psalms 17:1-15)

14 with your hand, O Lord, from human beings, from people whose portion in life is this world. You fill their stomachs with your treasure, their children will be satisfied too and will leave their wealth to their little ones 15 But I will see you, because I have done no wrong; and when I awake, your presence will fill me with joy. (Psalms 17:1-15)

A prayer of Jacob

9 And Jacob said, O God of my father Abraham, and God of my father Isaac, the Lord which saidst unto me, Return unto thy country, and to thy kindred, and I will deal well with thee: 10 I am not worthy of the least of all the mercies, and of all the truth, which thou hast shewed unto thy servant; for with my staff I passed over this Jordan; and now I am become two bands. 11 Deliver me, I pray thee, from the hand of my brother, from the hand of Esau: for I fear him, lest he will come and smite me, and the mother with the children. 12 And thou saidst, I will surely do thee good, and make thy seed as the sand of the sea, which cannot be numbered for multitude. (Genesis 32:9-12)

9 Then Jacob prayed, "God of my grandfather Abraham and God of my father Isaac, who told me, 'Return to your country and your kinsmen, and I will do you good'. 10 I am not worthy of all the kindness and faithfulness that you have shown me, your servant. I crossed the Jordan with nothing but a walking stick, and now I have come back with these two camps. 11 Save me, I pray, from my brother Esau. I'm afraid of him, afraid he'll come and attack me, without regard for mothers or children. 12 Remember that you promised to make everything go well for me and to give me more descendants than anyone could count, as many as the grains of sand along the seashore." (Genesis 32:9-12)

Prayer - Day 2

A prayer of David

1 Bow down thine ear, O Lord, hear me: for I am poor and needy. 2 Preserve my soul; for I am holy: O thou my God, save thy servant that trusteth in thee. 3 Be merciful unto me, O Lord: for I cry unto thee daily. 4 Rejoice the soul of thy servant: for unto thee, O Lord, do I lift up my soul. 5 For thou, Lord, art good, and ready to forgive; and plenteous in mercy unto all them that call upon thee. 6 Give ear, O Lord, unto my prayer; and attend to the voice of my supplications. 7 In the day of my trouble I will call upon thee: for thou wilt answer me. 8 Among the gods there is none like unto thee, O Lord; neither are there any works like unto thy works. 9 All nations whom thou hast made shall come and worship before thee, O Lord; and shall glorify thy name. 10 For thou art great, and doest wondrous things: thou art God alone. 11 Teach me thy way, O Lord; I will walk in thy truth: unite my heart to fear thy name. 12 I will praise thee, O Lord my God, with all my heart: and I will glorify thy name for evermore. 13 For great is thy mercy toward me: and thou hast delivered my soul from the lowest hell. 14 O God, the proud are risen against me, and the assemblies of violent men have sought after my soul; and have not set thee before them. 15 But thou, O Lord, art a God full of compassion, and gracious, long suffering, and plenteous in mercy and truth.

1 Listen to me, Lord, and answer me, for I am helpless and weak. 2 Save me from death, because I am loyal to you; save me, for I am your servant and I trust in you. 3 You are my God, so be merciful to me; I pray to you all day long. 4 Make your servant glad, O Lord, because my prayers go up to you. 5 You are good to us and forgiving, full of constant love for all who pray to you. 6 Listen, Lord, to my prayer; hear my cries for help. I call to you in times of trouble, because you answer my prayers. 8 There is no god like you, O Lord, not one has done what you have done. 9 All the nations that you have created will come and bow down to you; they will honor your name. 10 You are mighty and do wonderful things; you alone are God. 11 Teach me, Lord, what you want me to do, and I will obey you faithfully; teach me to serve you with complete devotion, so that I can fear your name. 12 I will praise you with all my heart, O Lord my God; I will proclaim your greatness forever. 13 How great is your constant love for me! You have saved me from lowest part of hell. 14 Proud people are coming against me, O God; a cruel gang is trying to kill me— people who pay no attention to you. 15 But you, O Lord, are a merciful and loving God, always patient, always kind and faithful.

16 O turn unto me, and have mercy upon me; give thy strength unto thy servant, and save the son of thine handmaid. 17 Shew me a token for good; that they which hate me may see it, and be ashamed: because thou, Lord, hast holpen me, and comforted me. (Psalms 86:1-17)

16 Turn to me and have mercy on me; strengthen me and save me, because I serve you just as my mother did. 17 Show me proof of your goodness, Lord; those who hate me will be ashamed when they see that you have given me comfort and help. (Psalms 86:1-17)

A prayer of the servant of Abraham

12 And he said O Lord God of my master Abraham, I pray thee, send me good speed this day, and shew kindness unto my master Abraham. 13 Behold, I stand here by the well of water; and the daughters of the men of the city come out to draw water: 14 And let it come to pass, that the damsel to whom I shall say, Let down thy pitcher, I pray thee, that I may drink; and she shall say, Drink, and I will give thy camels drink also: let the same be she that thou hast appointed for thy servant Isaac; and thereby shall I know that thou hast shewed kindness unto my master. (Genesis 24:12-14)

12 He said, "Lord, God of my master Abraham, please let me succeed today; and show your grace to my master Abraham. 13 Here I am, standing by the spring, as the daughters of the townsfolk come out to draw water. 14 I will say to one of the girls, 'Please lower your jug, so that I can drink.' If she answers, 'Yes, drink; and I will water your camels as well,' then let her be the one you intend for your servant Isaac. This is how I will know that you have shown grace to my master." (Genesis 24:12-14)

Prayer - Day 3

A prayer of Moses

1 Lord, thou hast been our dwelling place in all generations. 2 Before the mountains were brought forth, or ever thou hadst formed the earth and the world, even from everlasting to everlasting, thou art God. 3 Thou turnest man to destruction; and sayest, Return, ye children of men. 4 For a thousand years in thy sight are but as yesterday when it is past, and as a watch in the night. 5 Thou carriest them away as with a flood; they are as a sleep: in the morning they are like grass which groweth up. 6 In the morning it flourisheth, and groweth up; in the evening it is cut down, and withereth. 7 For we are consumed by thine anger, and by thy wrath are we troubled. 8 Thou hast set our iniquities before thee, our secret sins in the light of thy countenance. 9 For all our days are passed away in thy wrath: we spend our years as a tale that is told. 10 The days of our years are threescore years and ten; and if by reason of strength they be fourscore years, yet is their strength labour and sorrow; for it is soon cut off, and we fly away. 11 Who knoweth the power of thine anger? even according to thy fear, so is thy wrath. 12 So teach us to number our days, that we may apply our hearts unto wisdom. 13 Return, O Lord, how long? and let it repent thee concerning thy servants. 14 O satisfy us early with thy mercy; that we may rejoice and be glad all our days.

1 O Lord, you have always been our home in every generation. 2 Before you created the hills or brought the world into being, you were eternally God, and will be God forever. 3 You bring frail mortals to the point of being crushed, then say, "People, repent!" 4 A thousand years to you are like one day; they are like yesterday, already gone, like a short hour in the night. 5 You carry us away like a flood; we last no longer than a dream. We are like weeds that sprout in the morning, 6 that grow and burst into bloom, then dry up and die in the evening. 7 We are destroyed by your anger; we are terrified by your fury. 8 You place our sins before you, our secret sins where you can see them. 9 Our life is cut short by your anger; it fades away like a whisper. 10 Seventy years is all we have— eighty years, if we are strong; yet all they bring us is trouble and sorrow; life is soon over, and we are gone. 11 Who has felt the full power of your anger? Who knows what fear your fury can bring?
12 Teach us how short our life is, so that we may become wise. 13 How much longer will your anger last? Have pity, O Lord, on your servants! 14 Fill us each morning with your constant love, so that we may sing and be glad all our life.

15 Make us glad according to the days wherein thou hast afflicted us, and the years wherein we have seen evil. 16 Let thy work appear unto thy servants, and thy glory unto their children. 17 And let the beauty of the Lord our God be upon us: and establish thou the work of our hands upon us; yea, the work of our hands establish thou it. (Psalms 90:1-17)

15 Give us now as much happiness as the sadness you gave us during all our years of misery. 16 Let us, your servants, see your mighty deeds; let our descendants see your glorious might. 17 Lord our God, may your blessings be with us. Give us success in all we do!. (Psalms 90:1-17)

A prayer of Elijah the prophet

20 And he cried unto the Lord, and said, O Lord my God, hast thou also brought evil upon the widow with whom I sojourn, by slaying her son? 21 And he stretched himself upon the child three times, and cried unto the Lord, and said, O Lord my God, I pray thee, let this child's soul come into him again. 22 And the Lord heard the voice of Elijah; and the soul of the child came into him again, and he revived. (1 Kings 17:20-22)

20 Then he prayed aloud, "O Lord my God, Have you brought also this misery on the widow I'm staying with by killing her son?" 21 Then Elijah stretched himself out on the boy three times and prayed, "O Lord my God, restore this child to life!" 22 The Lord answered Elijah's prayer; the child started breathing again and revived. (1 Kings 17:20-22)

Prayer - Day 4

A prayer of the afflicted

1 Hear my prayer, O Lord, and let my cry come unto thee. 2 Hide not thy face from me in the day when I am in trouble; incline thine ear unto me: in the day when I call answer me speedily. 3 For my days are consumed like smoke, and my bones are burned as an hearth. 4 My heart is smitten, and withered like grass; so that I forget to eat my bread. 5 By reason of the voice of my groaning my bones cleave to my skin. 6 I am like a pelican of the wilderness: I am like an owl of the desert. 7 I watch, and am as a sparrow alone upon the house top. 8 Mine enemies reproach me all the day; and they that are mad against me are sworn against me. 9 For I have eaten ashes like bread, and mingled my drink with weeping. 10 Because of thine indignation and thy wrath: for thou hast lifted me up, and cast me down. 11 My days are like a shadow that declineth; and I am withered like grass. 12 But thou, O Lord, shall endure for ever; and thy remembrance unto all generations. 13 Thou shalt arise, and have mercy upon Zion: for the time to favour her, yea, the set time, is come. 14 For thy servants take pleasure in her stones, and favour the dust thereof. 15 So the heathen shall fear the name of the Lord, and all the kings of the earth thy glory. 16 When the Lord shall build up Zion, he shall appear in his glory. 17 He will regard the prayer of the destitute, and not despise their prayer.

1 Listen to my prayer, O Lord, and hear my cry for help!
2 When I am in trouble, don't turn away from me! Listen to me, and answer me quickly when I call! 3 My life is disappearing like smoke; my body is burning like fire. 4 I am beaten down like dry grass; I have lost my desire for food. 5 I groan aloud; I am nothing but skin and bones.
6 I am like a wild bird in the desert, like an owl in abandoned ruins. 7 I lie awake; I am like a lonely bird on a housetop. 8 All day long my enemies insult me; those who mock me use my name in cursing. 9-10 Because of your anger and fury, ashes are my food, and my tears are mixed with my drink. You picked me up and threw me away.
11 My life is like the evening shadows; I am like dry grass. 12 But you, O Lord, are king forever; all generations will remember you. 13 You will rise and take pity on Zion; the time has come to have mercy on her; this is the right time.
14 Your servants love her, even though she is destroyed;
they have pity on her, even though she is in ruins. 15 The nations will fear the Lord; all the kings of the earth will fear his power. 16 When the Lord rebuilds Zion, he will reveal his greatness. 17 He will hear his forsaken people and listen to their prayer.

18 This shall be written for the generation to come: and the people which shall be created shall praise the Lord. 19 For he hath looked down from the height of his sanctuary; from heaven did the Lord behold the earth; 20 To hear the groaning of the prisoner; to loose those that are appointed to death; 21 To declare the name of the Lord in Zion, and his praise in Jerusalem; 22 When the people are gathered together, and the kingdoms, to serve the Lord. 23 He weakened my strength in the way; he shortened my days. 24 I said, O my God, take me not away in the midst of my days: thy years are throughout all generations. 25 Of old hast thou laid the foundation of the earth: and the heavens are the work of thy hands. 26 They shall perish, but thou shalt endure: yea, all of them shall wax old like a garment; as a vesture shalt thou change them, and they shall be changed: 27 But thou art the same, and thy years shall have no end. 28 The children of thy servants shall continue, and their seed shall be established before thee. (Psalms 102:1-28)

18 Write down for the coming generation what the Lord has done, so that people not yet born will praise him. 19 The Lord looked down from his holy place on high, he looked down from heaven to earth. 20 He heard the groans of prisoners and set free those who were condemned to die. 21 And so his name will be proclaimed in Zion, and he will be praised in Jerusalem 22 when nations and kingdoms come together and worship the Lord. 23 The Lord has made me weak while I am still young; he has shortened my life. 24 O God, do not take me away now before I grow old. O Lord, you live forever; 25 long ago you created the earth, and with your own hands you made the heavens. 26 They will disappear, but you will remain; they will all wear out like clothes. You will discard them like clothes, and they will vanish. 27 But you are always the same, and your life never ends. 28 Our children will live in safety, and under your protection their descendants will be secure. (Psalms 102:1-28)

Prayer - Day 5

A prayer of David

1 I cried unto the Lord with my voice; with my voice unto the Lord did I make my supplication. 2 I poured out my complaint before him; I shewed before him my trouble. 3 When my spirit was overwhelmed within me, then thou knewest my path. In the way wherein I walked have they privily laid a snare for me. 4 I looked on my right hand, and beheld, but there was no man that would know me: refuge failed me; no man cared for my soul. 5 I cried unto thee, O Lord: I said, Thou art my refuge and my portion in the land of the living. 6 Attend unto my cry; for I am brought very low: deliver me from my persecutors; for they are stronger than I. 7 Bring my soul out of prison, that I may praise thy name: the righteous shall compass me about; for thou shalt deal bountifully with me. (Psalms 142:1-7)

1 I call to the Lord for help with my voice; with my voice I plead with him. 2 I bring him all my complaints; I tell him all my troubles. 3 When I am ready to give up, he knows what I should do. In the path where I walk, my enemies have hidden a trap for me. 4 When I look beside me, I see that there is no one to help me, no one to protect me. No one cares for me. 5 Lord, I cry to you for help; you, Lord, are my protector; you are all I want in this life. 6 Listen to my cry for help, for I am sunk in despair. Save me from my enemies; they are too strong for me. 7 Set me free from my distress; then in the assembly of your people I will praise your name because of your goodness to me. (Psalms 142:1-7)

A prayer of Hannah

9 So Hannah rose up after they had eaten in Shiloh, and after they had drunk. Now Eli the priest sat upon a seat by a post of the temple of the Lord. 10 And she was in bitterness of soul, and prayed unto the Lord, and wept sore. 11 And she vowed a vow, and said, O Lord of hosts, if thou wilt indeed look on the affliction of thine handmaid, and remember me, and not forget thine handmaid, but wilt give unto thine handmaid a man child, then I will give him unto the Lord all the days of his life, and there shall no razor come upon his head.

9 One time, after they had finished their meal in the house of the Lord at Shiloh, Hannah got up. She was deeply distressed, and she cried bitterly as she prayed to the Lord. Meanwhile, Eli the priest was sitting in his place by the door. 11 Hannah made a solemn promise: "Lord Almighty, look at me, your servant! See my trouble and remember me! Don't forget me! If you give me a son, I promise that I will dedicate him to you for his whole life and that he will never have his hair cut."

12 And it came to pass, as she continued praying before the Lord, that Eli marked her mouth. 13 Now Hannah, she spake in her heart; only her lips moved, but her voice was not heard: therefore Eli thought she had been drunken. 14 And Eli said unto her, How long wilt thou be drunken? put away thy wine from thee. 15 And Hannah answered and said, No, my lord, I am a woman of a sorrowful spirit: I have drunk neither wine nor strong drink, but have poured out my soul before the Lord. 16 Count not thine handmaid for a daughter of Belial: for out of the abundance of my complaint and grief have I spoken hitherto. 17 Then Eli answered and said, Go in peace: and the God of Israel grant thee thy petition that thou hast asked of him.18 And she said, Let thine handmaid find grace in thy sight. So the woman went her way, and did eat, and her countenance was no more sad. ([1 Samuel 1:9-18](#))

12 Hannah continued to pray to the Lord for a long time, and Eli watched her lips. 13 She was praying silently; her lips were moving, but she made no sound. So Eli thought that she was drunk, 14 and he said to her, "Stop making a drunken show of yourself Stop your drinking and sober up!" 15 "No, I'm not drunk, sir," she answered. "I haven't been drinking! I am desperate, and I have been praying, pouring out my troubles to the Lord. 16 Don't think I am a worthless woman. I have been praying like this because I'm so miserable." 17 "Go in peace," Eli said, "and may the God of Israel give you what you have asked him for." 18 "May you always think kindly of me," she replied. Then she went away, ate some food, and was no longer sad. ([1 Samuel 1:9-18](#))

Prayer - Day 6

A prayer of David after sin with Bathsheba

1 Have mercy upon me, O God, according to thy lovingkindness: according unto the multitude of thy tender mercies blot out my transgressions. 2 Wash me throughly from mine iniquity, and cleanse me from my sin. 3 For I acknowledge my transgressions: and my sin is ever before me. 4 Against thee, thee only, have I sinned, and done this evil in thy sight: that thou mightest be justified when thou speakest, and be clear when thou judgest. 5 Behold, I was shapen in iniquity; and in sin did my mother conceive me. 6 Behold, thou desirest truth in the inward parts: and in the hidden part thou shalt make me to know wisdom. 7 Purge me with hyssop, and I shall be clean: wash me, and I shall be whiter than snow. 8 Make me to hear joy and gladness; that the bones which thou hast broken may rejoice. 9 Hide thy face from my sins, and blot out all mine iniquities. 10 Create in me a clean heart, O God; and renew a right spirit within me. 11 Cast me not away from thy presence; and take not thy holy spirit from me. 12 Restore unto me the joy of thy salvation; and uphold me with thy free spirit. 13 Then will I teach transgressors thy ways; and sinners shall be converted unto thee. 14 Deliver me from bloodguiltiness, O God, thou God of my salvation: and my tongue shall sing aloud of thy righteousness. 15 O Lord, open thou my lips; and my mouth shall shew forth thy praise.

1 Be merciful to me, O God, because of your constant love. Because of your great mercy wipe away my sins! 2 Wash away all my evil and make me clean from my sin! 3 I recognize my faults; I am always conscious of my sins. 4 I have sinned against you—only against you— and done what you consider evil. So you are right in judging me; you are justified in condemning me. 5 I have been evil from the day I was born; from the time I was conceived, I have been sinful. 6 Sincerity and truth are what you require; fill my mind with your wisdom. 7 Remove my sin, and I will be clean; wash me, and I will be whiter than snow. 8 Let me hear the sounds of joy and gladness; and though you have crushed me and broken me, I will be happy once again. 9 Turn away your face from my sins and wipe out all my evil. 10 Create a pure heart in me, O God, and put a new and loyal spirit in me. 11 Do not banish me from your presence; do not take your holy spirit away from me. 12 Give me again the joy that comes from your salvation, and make me willing to obey you. 13 Then I will teach sinners your commands, and they will turn back to you. 14 Spare my life, O God, and save me, and I will gladly proclaim your righteousness. 15 Help me to speak, Lord, and I will praise you.

16 For thou desirest not sacrifice; else would I give it: thou delightest not in burnt offering. 17 The sacrifices of God are a broken spirit: a broken and a contrite heart, O God, thou wilt not despise. 18 Do good in thy good pleasure unto Zion: build thou the walls of Jerusalem. 19 Then shalt thou be pleased with the sacrifices of righteousness, with burnt offering and whole burnt offering: then shall they offer bullocks upon thine altar. (Psalms 51:1-19)

16 You do not want sacrifices, or I would offer them; you are not pleased with burnt offerings. 17 My sacrifice is a humble spirit, O God; you will not reject a humble and repentant heart. 18 O God, be kind to Zion and help her; rebuild the walls of Jerusalem. 19 Then you will be pleased with proper sacrifices and with our burnt offerings; and bulls will be sacrificed on your altar. (Psalms 51:1-19)

A prayer of Elijah the prophet

36 And it came to pass at the time of the offering of the evening sacrifice, that Elijah the prophet came near, and said, Lord God of Abraham, Isaac, and of Israel, let it be known this day that thou art God in Israel, and that I am thy servant, and that I have done all these things at thy word. 37 Hear me, O Lord, hear me, that this people may know that thou art the Lord God, and that thou hast turned their heart back again. 38 Then the fire of the Lord fell, and consumed the burnt sacrifice, and the wood, and the stones, and the dust, and licked up the water that was in the trench. 39 And when all the people saw it, they fell on their faces: and they said, The Lord, he is the God; the Lord, he is the God.(1 Kings 18:36-39)

36 At the hour of the afternoon sacrifice the prophet Elijah approached the altar and prayed, "O Lord, the God of Abraham, Isaac, and Jacob, prove now that you are the God of Israel and that I am your servant and have done all this at your command. 37 Answer me, Lord, answer me, so that this people will know that you, the Lord, are God and that you are bringing them back to yourself." 38 The Lord sent fire down, and it burned up the sacrifice, the wood, and the stones, scorched the earth and dried up the water in the trench. 39 When the people saw this, they threw themselves on the ground and exclaimed, "The Lord is God; the Lord alone is God!"(1 Kings 18:36-39)

Prayer - Day 7

A prayer of David

1 How long wilt thou forget me, O Lord? for ever? how long wilt thou hide thy face from me? 2 How long shall I take counsel in my soul, having sorrow in my heart daily? how long shall mine enemy be exalted over me? 3 Consider and hear me, O Lord my God: lighten mine eyes, lest I sleep the sleep of death; 4 Lest mine enemy say, I have prevailed against him; and those that trouble me rejoice when I am moved. 5 But I have trusted in thy mercy; my heart shall rejoice in thy salvation. 6 I will sing unto the Lord, because he hath dealt bountifully with me. (Psalms 13:1-6)

1 How much longer will you forget me, Lord? Forever? How much longer will you hide yourself from me? 2 How long must I endure trouble? How long will sorrow fill my heart day and night? How long will my enemies triumph over me? 3 Look, and answer me, O Lord my God. Restore my strength; don't let me die. 4 Don't let my enemies say, "We have defeated him." Don't let them gloat over my downfall. 5 I rely on your constant love; I will be glad, because you will rescue me. 6 I will sing to you, O Lord, because you have been good to me. (Psalms 13:1-6)

A prayer of Hannah

1 And Hannah prayed, and said, My heart rejoiceth in the Lord, mine horn is exalted in the Lord: my mouth is enlarged over mine enemies; because I rejoice in thy salvation. 2 There is none holy as the Lord: for there is none beside thee: neither is there any rock like our God. 3 Talk no more so exceedingly proudly; let not arrogancy come out of your mouth: for the Lord is a God of knowledge, and by him actions are weighed. 4 The bows of the mighty men are broken, and they that stumbled are girded with strength.

1 Hannah prayed: "The Lord has filled my heart with joy; how happy I am because of what he has done! I laugh at my enemies; how joyful I am because God has helped me! 2 "No one is holy like the Lord; there is none like him, no protector like our God. 3 Stop your loud boasting; silence your proud words. For the Lord is a God who knows, and he judges all that people do. 4 The bows of strong soldiers are broken, but the weak grow strong.

5 They that were full have hired out themselves for bread; and they that were hungry ceased: so that the barren hath born seven; and she that hath many children is waxed feeble. 6 The Lord killeth, and maketh alive: he bringeth down to the grave, and bringeth up. 7 The Lord maketh poor, and maketh rich: he bringeth low, and lifteth up. 8 He raiseth up the poor out of the dust, and lifteth up the beggar from the dunghill, to set them among princes, and to make them inherit the throne of glory: for the pillars of the earth are the Lord's, and he hath set the world upon them. 9 He will keep the feet of his saints, and the wicked shall be silent in darkness; for by strength shall no man prevail. 10 The adversaries of the Lord shall be broken to pieces; out of heaven shall he thunder upon them: the Lord shall judge the ends of the earth; and he shall give strength unto his king, and exalt the horn of his anointed. 11 And Elkanah went to Ramah to his house. And the child did minister unto the Lord before Eli the priest. ([1 Samuel 2:1-11](#))	5 The people who once were well fed now hire themselves out to get food, but the hungry are hungry no more. The childless wife has borne seven children, but the mother of many is left with none. 6 The Lord kills and restores to life; he sends people to the world of the dead and brings them back again. 7 He makes some people poor and others rich; he humbles some and makes others great. 8 He lifts the poor from the dust and raises the needy from their misery. He makes them companions of princes and puts them in places of honor. The foundations of the earth belong to the Lord; on them he has built the world. 9 "He protects the lives of his faithful people, but the wicked disappear in darkness; a man does not triumph by his own strength. 10 The Lord's enemies will be destroyed; he will thunder against them from heaven. The Lord will judge the whole world; he will give power to his king, he will make his chosen king victorious." 11 Then Elkanah went back home to Ramah, but the boy Samuel stayed in Shiloh and served the Lord under the priest Eli. ([1 Samuel 2:1-11](#))

Prayer - Day 8

A prayer of David

1 Judge me, O Lord; for I have walked in mine integrity: I have trusted also in the Lord; therefore I shall not slide. 2 Examine me, O Lord, and prove me; try my reins and my heart. 3 For thy lovingkindness is before mine eyes: and I have walked in thy truth. 4 I have not sat with vain persons, neither will I go in with dissemblers. 5 I have hated the congregation of evil doers; and will not sit with the wicked. 6 I will wash mine hands in innocency: so will I compass thine altar, O Lord: 7 That I may publish with the voice of thanksgiving, and tell of all thy wondrous works. 8 Lord, I have loved the habitation of thy house, and the place where thine honour dwelleth. 9 Gather not my soul with sinners, nor my life with bloody men: 10 In whose hands is mischief, and their right hand is full of bribes. 11 But as for me, I will walk in mine integrity: redeem me, and be merciful unto me. 12 My foot standeth in an even place: in the congregations will I bless the Lord. (Psalms 26:1-12)

1 Declare me innocent, O Lord, because I do what is right and trust you completely. 2 Examine me and test me, Lord; judge my desires and thoughts. 3 Your constant love is my guide; your faithfulness always leads me. 4 I do not keep company with worthless people; I have nothing to do with hypocrites. 5 I hate the company of the evil and avoid the wicked. 6 Lord, I wash my hands to show that I am innocent and march in worship around your altar. 7 I sing a hymn of thanksgiving and tell of all your wonderful deeds. 8 I love the house where you live, O Lord, the place where your glory abides. 9 Do not destroy me with the sinners; spare me from the fate of murderers— 10 those who do evil all the time and are always ready to take bribes. 11 As for me, I do what is right; be merciful to me and save me! 12 My feet are planted on level ground; in the assembly of his people I praise the Lord. (Psalms 26:1-12)

A prayer of Stephen

55 But he, being full of the Holy Ghost, looked up stedfastly into heaven, and saw the glory of God, and Jesus standing on the right hand of God, 56 And said, Behold, I see the heavens opened, and the Son of man standing on the right hand of God.

55 But Stephen, full of the Holy Spirit, looked up to heaven and saw God's glory and Jesus standing at the right hand of God. 56 "Look!" he said. "I see heaven opened and the Son of Man standing at the right hand of God!"

57 Then they cried out with a loud voice, and stopped their ears, and ran upon him with one accord, 58 And cast him out of the city, and stoned him: and the witnesses laid down their clothes at a young man's feet, whose name was Saul. 59 And they stoned Stephen, calling upon God, and saying, Lord Jesus, receive my spirit. 60 And he kneeled down, and cried with a loud voice, Lord, lay not this sin to their charge. And when he had said this, he fell asleep. (Acts 7:55-60)

57 With a loud cry the Council members covered their ears with their hands. Then they all rushed at him at once, 58 threw him out of the city, and stoned him. The witnesses left their cloaks in the care of a young man named Saul. 59 They kept on stoning Stephen as he called out to the Lord, "Lord Jesus, receive my spirit!" 60 He knelt down and cried out in a loud voice, "Lord! Do not remember this sin against them!" He said this and died. (Acts 7:55-60)

Prayer - Day 9

A prayer of David

1 In thee, O Lord, do I put my trust; let me never be ashamed: deliver me in thy righteousness. 2 Bow down thine ear to me; deliver me speedily: be thou my strong rock, for an house of defence to save me. 3 For thou art my rock and my fortress; therefore for thy name's sake lead me, and guide me. 4 Pull me out of the net that they have laid privily for me: for thou art my strength. 5 Into thine hand I commit my spirit: thou hast redeemed me, O Lord God of truth. 6 I have hated them that regard lying vanities: but I trust in the Lord. 7 I will be glad and rejoice in thy mercy: for thou hast considered my trouble; thou hast known my soul in adversities; 8 And hast not shut me up into the hand of the enemy: thou hast set my feet in a large room. 9 Have mercy upon me, O Lord, for I am in trouble: mine eye is consumed with grief, yea, my soul and my belly. 10 For my life is spent with grief, and my years with sighing: my strength faileth because of mine iniquity, and my bones are consumed. 11 I was a reproach among all mine enemies, but especially among my neighbours, and a fear to mine acquaintance: they that did see me without fled from me. 12 I am forgotten as a dead man out of mind: I am like a broken vessel. 13 For I have heard the slander of many: fear was on every side: while they took counsel together against me, they devised to take away my life.

1 I come to you, Lord, for protection; never let me be defeated. You are a righteous God; save me, I pray! 2 Hear me! Save me now! Be my refuge to protect me; my defense to save me. 3 You are my refuge and defense; for your name's sake guide me and lead me as you have promised. 4 Keep me safe from the trap that has been set for me; you are my shelter from danger. 5 I place myself in your care. You will save me, Lord; you are a faithful God. 6 I hate those who worship false gods, but I trust in you. 7 I will be glad and rejoice because of your constant love. You see my suffering; you know my trouble. 8 You have not let my enemies capture me; you have given me freedom to go where I wish. 9 Be merciful to me, Lord, for I am in trouble; my eyes are tired from so much crying; I am completely worn out. 10 I am exhausted by sorrow, and weeping has shortened my life. I am weak from all my troubles; even my bones are wasting away. 11 All my enemies, and especially my neighbors, treat me with contempt. Those who know me are afraid of me; when they see me in the street, they run away. 12 Everyone has forgotten me, as though I were dead; I am like something thrown away. 13 I hear many enemies whispering; terror is all around me. They are making plans against me, plotting to kill me.

14 But I trusted in thee, O Lord: I said, Thou art my God. 15 My times are in thy hand: deliver me from the hand of mine enemies, and from them that persecute me. 16 Make thy face to shine upon thy servant: save me for thy mercies' sake. 17 Let me not be ashamed, O Lord; for I have called upon thee: let the wicked be ashamed, and let them be silent in the grave. 18 Let the lying lips be put to silence; which speak grievous things proudly and contemptuously against the righteous. 19 Oh how great is thy goodness, which thou hast laid up for them that fear thee; which thou hast wrought for them that trust in thee before the sons of men! 20 Thou shalt hide them in the secret of thy presence from the pride of man: thou shalt keep them secretly in a pavilion from the strife of tongues. 21 Blessed be the Lord: for he hath shewed me his marvellous kindness in a strong city. 22 For I said in my haste, I am cut off from before thine eyes: nevertheless thou heardest the voice of my supplications when I cried unto thee. 23 O love the Lord, all ye his saints: for the Lord preserveth the faithful, and plentifully rewardeth the proud doer. 24 Be of good courage, and he shall strengthen your heart, all ye that hope in the Lord. (Psalms 31:1-24)

14 But my trust is in you, O Lord; you are my God. 15 I am always in your care; save me from my enemies, from those who persecute me. 16 Look on your servant with kindness; save me in your constant love. 17 I call to you, Lord; don't let me be disgraced. May the wicked be disgraced; may they go silently down to the world of the dead. 18 Silence those liars— all the proud and arrogant who speak with contempt about the righteous. 19 How wonderful are the good things you keep for those who honor you! Everyone knows how good you are, how securely you protect those who trust you. 20 You hide them in the safety of your presence from the plots of others; in a safe shelter you hide them from the insults of their enemies. 21 Praise the Lord! How wonderfully he showed his love for me when I was surrounded and attacked! 22 I was afraid and thought that he had driven me out of his presence. But he heard my cry, when I called to him for help. 23 Love the Lord, all his faithful people. The Lord protects the faithful, but punishes the proud as they deserve. 24 Be strong, be courageous, all you that hope in the Lord. (Psalms 31:1-24)

Prayer - Day 10

A prayer of David

1 O Lord, rebuke me not in thy wrath: neither chasten me in thy hot displeasure. 2 For thine arrows stick fast in me, and thy hand presseth me sore. 3 There is no soundness in my flesh because of thine anger; neither is there any rest in my bones because of my sin. 4 For mine iniquities are gone over mine head: as an heavy burden they are too heavy for me. 5 My wounds stink and are corrupt because of my foolishness. 6 I am troubled; I am bowed down greatly; I go mourning all the day long. 7 For my loins are filled with a loathsome disease: and there is no soundness in my flesh. 8 I am feeble and sore broken: I have roared by reason of the disquietness of my heart. 9 Lord, all my desire is before thee; and my groaning is not hid from thee. 10 My heart panteth, my strength faileth me: as for the light of mine eyes, it also is gone from me. 11 My lovers and my friends stand aloof from my sore; and my kinsmen stand afar off. 12 They also that seek after my life lay snares for me: and they that seek my hurt speak mischievous things, and imagine deceits all the day long. 13 But I, as a deaf man, heard not; and I was as a dumb man that openeth not his mouth. 14 Thus I was as a man that heareth not, and in whose mouth are no reproofs. 15 For in thee, O Lord, do I hope: thou wilt hear, O Lord my God. 16 For I said, Hear me, lest otherwise they should rejoice over me: when my foot slippeth, they magnify themselves against me.

1 O Lord, don't punish me in your anger! 2 You have wounded me with your arrows; you have struck me down. 3 Because of your anger, I am in great pain; my whole body is diseased because of my sins. 4 I am drowning in the flood of my sins; they are a burden too heavy to bear. 5 Because I have been foolish, my sores stink and rot. 6 I am bent over, I am crushed; I mourn all day long. 7 I am burning with fever and I am near death. 8 I am worn out and utterly crushed; my heart is troubled, and I groan with pain. 9 O Lord, you know what I long for; you hear all my groans. 10 My heart is pounding, my strength is gone, and my eyes have lost their brightness. 11 My friends and neighbors will not come near me, because of my sores; even my family keeps away from me. 12 Those who want to kill me lay traps for me, and those who want to hurt me threaten to ruin me; they never stop plotting against me. 13 I am like the deaf and cannot hear, like the dumb and cannot speak. 14 I am like those who do not answer, because they cannot hear. 15 But I trust in you, O Lord; and you, O Lord my God, will answer me. 16 Don't let my enemies gloat over my distress; don't let them boast about my downfall!

17 For I am ready to halt, and my sorrow is continually before me. 18 For I will declare mine iniquity; I will be sorry for my sin. 19 But mine enemies are lively, and they are strong: and they that hate me wrongfully are multiplied. 20 They also that render evil for good are mine adversaries; because I follow the thing that good is. 21 Forsake me not, O Lord: O my God, be not far from me. 22 Make haste to help me, O Lord my salvation. (Psalms 38:1-22)

17 I am about to fall and am in constant pain. 18 I confess my sins; they fill me with anxiety. 19 My enemies are healthy and strong; there are many who hate me for no reason. 20 Those who pay back evil for good are against me because I try to do right. 21 Do not abandon me, O Lord; do not stay away, my God! 22 Help me now, O Lord my savior!. (Psalms 38:1-22)

A prayer of Hezekiah

15 And Hezekiah prayed before the Lord, and said, O Lord God of Israel, which dwellest between the cherubims, thou art the God, even thou alone, of all the kingdoms of the earth; thou hast made heaven and earth. 16 Lord, bow down thine ear, and hear: open, Lord, thine eyes, and see: and hear the words of Sennacherib, which hath sent him to reproach the living God. 17 Of a truth, Lord, the kings of Assyria have destroyed the nations and their lands, 18 And have cast their gods into the fire: for they were no gods, but the work of men's hands, wood and stone: therefore they have destroyed them. 19 Now therefore, O Lord our God, I beseech thee, save thou us out of his hand, that all the kingdoms of the earth may know that thou art the Lord God, even thou only.

(2 Kings 19:15-19)

15 and Hezekiah prayed, "O Lord, the God of Israel, seated on your throne above the winged cheribims, you alone are God, ruling all the kingdoms of the world. You created the earth and the sky. 16 Now, Lord, look at what is happening to us. Listen to all the things that Sennacherib is saying to insult you, the living God. 17 We all know, Lord, that the emperors of Assyria have destroyed many nations, made their lands desolate, 18 and burned up their gods—which were no gods at all, only images of wood and stone made by human hands. 19 Now, Lord our God, rescue us from the Assyrians, so that all the nations of the world will know that only you, O Lord, are God." (2 Kings 19:15-19)

Prayer - Day 11

A prayer of David

1 Make haste, O God, to deliver me; make haste to help me, O Lord. 2 Let them be ashamed and confounded that seek after my soul: let them be turned backward, and put to confusion, that desire my hurt. 3 Let them be turned back for a reward of their shame that say, Aha, aha. 4 Let all those that seek thee rejoice and be glad in thee: and let such as love thy salvation say continually, Let God be magnified. 5 But I am poor and needy: make haste unto me, O God: thou art my help and my deliverer; O Lord, make no tarrying. (Psalms 70:1-5)

1 Save me, O God! Lord, help me now! 2 May those who try to kill me be defeated and confused. May those who are happy because of my troubles be turned back and disgraced. 3 May those who make fun of me be dismayed by their defeat. 4 May all who come to you be glad and joyful. May all who are thankful for your salvation always say, "How great is God!" 5 I am weak and poor; come to me quickly, O God. You are my helper and rescuer; O Lord, don't delay! (Psalms 70:1-5)

A prayer of Solomon

5 In Gibeon the Lord appeared to Solomon in a dream by night: and God said, Ask what I shall give thee. 6 And Solomon said, Thou hast shewed unto thy servant David my father great mercy, according as he walked before thee in truth, and in righteousness, and in uprightness of heart with thee; and thou hast kept for him this great kindness, that thou hast given him a son to sit on his throne, as it is this day. 7 And now, O Lord my God, thou hast made thy servant king instead of David my father: and I am but a little child: I know not how to go out or come in. 8 And thy servant is in the midst of thy people which thou hast chosen, a great people, that cannot be numbered nor counted for multitude.

5 I Gideon the Lord appeared to Solomon in a dream at night and asked him, "What would you like me to give you?" 6 Solomon answered, "You always showed great love for my father David, your servant, and he was good, loyal, and honest in his relation with you. And you have continued to show him your great and constant love by giving him a son who today rules in his place. 7 O Lord God, you have let me succeed my father as king, even though I am very young and don't know how to rule. 8 Here I am among the people you have chosen to be your own, a people who are so many that they cannot be counted.

9 Give therefore thy servant an understanding heart to judge thy people, that I may discern between good and bad: for who is able to judge this thy so great a people? 10 And the speech pleased the Lord, that Solomon had asked this thing. 11 And God said unto him, Because thou hast asked this thing, and hast not asked for thyself long life; neither hast asked riches for thyself, nor hast asked the life of thine enemies; but hast asked for thyself understanding to discern judgment; 12 Behold, I have done according to thy words: lo, I have given thee a wise and an understanding heart; so that there was none like thee before thee, neither after thee shall any arise like unto thee. 13 And I have also given thee that which thou hast not asked, both riches, and honour: so that there shall not be any among the kings like unto thee all thy days. 14 And if thou wilt walk in my ways, to keep my statutes and my commandments, as thy father David did walk, then I will lengthen thy days. 15 And Solomon awoke; and, behold, it was a dream. And he came to Jerusalem, and stood before the ark of the covenant of the Lord, and offered up burnt offerings, and offered peace offerings, and made a feast to all his servants.

(1 Kings 3:5-15)

9 So give me the wisdom I need to rule your people with justice and to know the difference between good and evil. Otherwise, how would I ever be able to rule this great people of yours?" 10 The Lord was pleased that Solomon had asked for this, 11 and so he said to him, "Because you have asked for the wisdom to rule justly, instead of long life for yourself or riches or the death of your enemies, 12 I will do what you have asked. I will give you more wisdom and understanding than anyone has ever had before or will ever have again. 13 I will also give you what you have not asked for: all your life you will have wealth and honor, more than that of any other king. 14 And if you obey me and keep my laws and commands, as your father David did, I will give you a long life."

15 Solomon woke up and realized that God had spoken to him in the dream. Then he went to Jerusalem and stood in front of the ark of the Covenant of the Lord and offered burnt offerings and fellowship offerings to the Lord. After that he gave a feast for all his officials. (1 Kings 3:5-15)

Prayer - Day 12

Prayer of David

1 In thee, O Lord, do I put my trust: let me never be put to confusion. 2 Deliver me in thy righteousness, and cause me to escape: incline thine ear unto me, and save me. 3 Be thou my strong habitation, whereunto I may continually resort: thou hast given commandment to save me; for thou art my rock and my fortress. 4 Deliver me, O my God, out of the hand of the wicked, out of the hand of the unrighteous and cruel man. 5 For thou art my hope, O Lord God: thou art my trust from my youth. 6 By thee have I been holden up from the womb: thou art he that took me out of my mother's bowels: my praise shall be continually of thee. 7 I am as a wonder unto many; but thou art my strong refuge. 8 Let my mouth be filled with thy praise and with thy honour all the day. 9 Cast me not off in the time of old age; forsake me not when my strength faileth. 10 For mine enemies speak against me; and they that lay wait for my soul take counsel together, 11 Saying, God hath forsaken him: persecute and take him; for there is none to deliver him. 12 O God, be not far from me: O my God, make haste for my help. 13 Let them be confounded and consumed that are adversaries to my soul; let them be covered with reproach and dishonour that seek my hurt. 14 But I will hope continually, and will yet praise thee more and more.

1 Lord, I have come to you for protection; never let me be defeated! 2 Because you are righteous, help me and rescue me. Turn your ear toward me and save me! 3 Be my secure shelter and a strong fortress to protect me; you are my refuge and defense. 4 My God, rescue me from wicked people, from the power of cruel and evil people. 5 Sovereign Lord, I put my hope in you; I have trusted in you since I was young. 6 I have relied on you all my life; you have protected me since the day I was born. I will always praise you. 7 My life has been an example to many, because you have been my strong defender. 8 All day long I praise you and proclaim your glory. 9 Do not reject me now that I am old; do not abandon me now that I am feeble. 10 My enemies want to kill me; they talk and plot against me. 11 They say, "God has abandoned him; let's go after him and catch him; there is no one to rescue him." 12 Don't stay so far away, O God; my God, hurry to my aid! 13 May those who attack me be defeated and destroyed. May those who try to hurt me be shamed and disgraced. 14 I will always put my hope in you; I will praise you more and more.

15 My mouth shall shew forth thy righteousness and thy salvation all the day; for I know not the numbers thereof. 16 I will go in the strength of the Lord God: I will make mention of thy righteousness, even of thine only. 17 O God, thou hast taught me from my youth: and hitherto have I declared thy wondrous works. 18 Now also when I am old and greyheaded, O God, forsake me not; until I have shewed thy strength unto this generation, and thy power to every one that is to come. 19 Thy righteousness also, O God, is very high, who hast done great things: O God, who is like unto thee! 20 Thou, which hast shewed me great and sore troubles, shalt quicken me again, and shalt bring me up again from the depths of the earth. 21 Thou shalt increase my greatness, and comfort me on every side. 22 I will also praise thee with the psaltery, even thy truth, O my God: unto thee will I sing with the harp, O thou Holy One of Israel. 23 My lips shall greatly rejoice when I sing unto thee; and my soul, which thou hast redeemed. 24 My tongue also shall talk of thy righteousness all the day long: for they are confounded, for they are brought unto shame, that seek my hurt. (Psalms 71:1-24)

15 I will tell of your goodness; all day long I will speak of your salvation, though it is more than I can understand. 16 I will go in the strength of the Lord God; I will proclaim your goodness, yours alone. 17 You have taught me ever since I was young, and I still tell of your wonderful acts. 18 Now that I am old and my hair is gray, do not abandon me, O God! Be with me while I proclaim your power and might to all generations to come. 19 Your righteousness, God, reaches the skies. You have done great things; there is no one like you. 20 You have sent troubles and suffering on me, but you will restore my strength; you will keep me from the grave. 21 You will make me greater than ever; you will comfort me again. 22 I will indeed praise you with the harp; I will praise your faithfulness, my God. On my harp I will play hymns to you, the Holy One of Israel. 23 I will shout for joy as I play for you; with my whole being I will sing because you have saved me. 24 I will speak of your righteousness all day long, because those who tried to harm me have been defeated and disgraced.. (Psalms 71:1-24)

Prayer - Day 13

A prayer of David

1 Lord, I cry unto thee: make haste unto me; give ear unto my voice, when I cry unto thee. 2 Let my prayer be set forth before thee as incense; and the lifting up of my hands as the evening sacrifice. 3 Set a watch, O Lord, before my mouth; keep the door of my lips. 4 Incline not my heart to any evil thing, to practise wicked works with men that work iniquity: and let me not eat of their dainties. 5 Let the righteous smite me; it shall be a kindness: and let him reprove me; it shall be an excellent oil, which shall not break my head: for yet my prayer also shall be in their calamities. 6 When their judges are overthrown in stony places, they shall hear my words; for they are sweet. 7 Our bones are scattered at the grave's mouth, as when one cutteth and cleaveth wood upon the earth. 8 But mine eyes are unto thee, O God the Lord: in thee is my trust; leave not my soul destitute. 9 Keep me from the snares which they have laid for me, and the gins of the workers of iniquity. 10 Let the wicked fall into their own nets, whilst that I withal escape. (Psalms 141:1-10)

1 I call to you, Lord; help me now! Listen to my plea when I call to you. 2 Receive my prayer as incense, my uplifted hands as an evening sacrifice. 3 Lord, place a guard at my mouth, a sentry at the door of my lips. 4 Keep me from wanting to do wrong and from joining evil people in their wickedness. May I never take part in their feasts. 5 Good people may punish me and rebuke me in kindness, but I will never accept honor from evil people, because I am always praying against their evil deeds. 6 When their rulers are thrown down from rocky cliffs, the people will admit that my words were true. 7 Like wood that is split and chopped into bits, so their bones are scattered at the edge of the grave. 8 But I keep trusting in you, my Sovereign Lord. I seek your protection; don't let me die! 9 Protect me from the traps they have set for me, from the snares of those evildoers. 10 May the wicked fall into their own traps while I go by unharmed. (Psalms 14:1-10)

A prayer of David

1 Hear my prayer, O Lord, give ear to my supplications: in thy faithfulness answer me, and in thy righteousness. 2 And enter not into judgment with thy servant: for in thy sight shall no man living be justified.

1 Lord, hear my prayer! In your righteousness listen to my plea; answer me in your faithfulness! 2 Don't put me, your servant, on trial; no one is innocent in your sight.

3 For the enemy hath persecuted my soul; he hath smitten my life down to the ground; he hath made me to dwell in darkness, as those that have been long dead. 4 Therefore is my spirit overwhelmed within me; my heart within me is desolate. 5 I remember the days of old; I meditate on all thy works; I muse on the work of thy hands. 6 I stretch forth my hands unto thee: my soul thirsteth after thee, as a thirsty land. Selah. 7 Hear me speedily, O Lord: my spirit faileth: hide not thy face from me, lest I be like unto them that go down into the pit. 8 Cause me to hear thy lovingkindness in the morning; for in thee do I trust: cause me to know the way wherein I should walk; for I lift up my soul unto thee. 9 Deliver me, O Lord, from mine enemies: I flee unto thee to hide me. 10 Teach me to do thy will; for thou art my God: thy spirit is good; lead me into the land of uprightness. 11 Quicken me, O Lord, for thy name's sake: for thy righteousness' sake bring my soul out of trouble. 12 And of thy mercy cut off mine enemies, and destroy all them that afflict my soul: for I am thy servant. (Psalms 143:1-12)

3 My enemies have hunted me down and completely defeated me. They have put me in a dark prison, and I am like those who died long ago. 4 So I am ready to give up; I am in deep despair. 5 I remember the days gone by; I think about all that you have done, I bring to mind all your deeds. 6 I lift up my hands to you in prayer; like dry ground my soul is thirsty for you. 7 Answer me now, Lord! I have lost all hope. Don't hide yourself from me, or I'll be like those who drop down into a pit. 8 Remind me each morning of your constant love, for I put my trust in you. My prayers go up to you; show me the way I should go. 9 I go to you for protection, Lord; rescue me from my enemies. 10 You are my God; teach me to do your will. Let your good Spirit guide me on a safe path. 11 Rescue me, Lord, as you have promised; in your goodness and for your name's sake save me from my troubles! 12 Because of your love for me, cut off my enemies and destroy all my oppressors, for I am your servant. (Psalms 143:1-12)

Prayer - Day 14

A prayer of Moses

25 Thus I fell down before the Lord forty days and forty nights, as I fell down at the first; because the Lord had said he would destroy you. 26 I prayed therefore unto the Lord, and said, O Lord God, destroy not thy people and thine inheritance, which thou hast redeemed through thy greatness, which thou hast brought forth out of Egypt with a mighty hand. 27 Remember thy servants, Abraham, Isaac, and Jacob; look not unto the stubbornness of this people, nor to their wickedness, nor to their sin: 28 Lest the land whence thou broughtest us out say, Because the Lord was not able to bring them into the land which he promised them, and because he hated them, he hath brought them out to slay them in the wilderness. 29 Yet they are thy people and thine inheritance, which thou broughtest out by thy mighty power and by thy stretched out arm.
(Deuteronomy 9:25-29)

25 "So I lay face downward in the Lord's presence those forty days and nights, because I knew that he was determined to destroy you. 26 And I prayed, 'Sovereign Lord, don't destroy your own people, the people you rescued and brought out of Egypt by your great strength and power. 27 Remember your servants, Abraham, Isaac, and Jacob, and do not pay any attention to the stubbornness, wickedness, and sin of this people. 28 Otherwise, the Egyptians will say that you were unable to take your people into the land that you had promised them. They will say that you took your people out into the desert to kill them, because you hated them. 29 After all, these are the people whom you chose to be your own and whom you brought out of Egypt by your great power and might.'
(Deuteronomy 9:25-29)

A prayer of Hezekiah

1 In those days was Hezekiah sick unto death. And the prophet Isaiah the son of Amoz came to him, and said unto him, Thus saith the Lord, Set thine house in order; for thou shalt die, and not live. 2 Then he turned his face to the wall, and prayed unto the Lord, saying,

1 About this time King Hezekiah became sick and almost died. The prophet Isaiah son of Amoz went to see him and said to him, "The Lord tells you that you are to put everything in order, because you will not recover. Get ready to die." 2 Hezekiah turned his face to the wall and prayed:

3 I beseech thee, O Lord, remember now how I have walked before thee in truth and with a perfect heart, and have done that which is good in thy sight. And Hezekiah wept sore. 4 And it came to pass, afore Isaiah was gone out into the middle court, that the word of the Lord came to him, saying, 5 Turn again, and tell Hezekiah the captain of my people, Thus saith the Lord, the God of David thy father, I have heard thy prayer, I have seen thy tears: behold, I will heal thee: on the third day thou shalt go up unto the house of the Lord. 6 And I will add unto thy days fifteen years; and I will deliver thee and this city out of the hand of the king of Assyria; and I will defend this city for mine own sake, and for my servant David's sake. (2 Kings 20:1-6)

3 "Remember, Lord, that I have served you faithfully and loyally and that I have always tried to do what you wanted me to." And he began to cry bitterly. 4 Isaiah left the king, but before he had passed through the central courtyard of the palace the Lord told him 5 to go back to Hezekiah, ruler of the Lord's people, and say to him, "I, the Lord, the God of your ancestor David, have heard your prayer and seen your tears. I will heal you, and in three days you will go to the Temple. 6 I will let you live fifteen years longer. I will rescue you and this city Jerusalem from the emperor of Assyria. I will defend this city, for the sake of my own honor and because of the promise I made to my servant David." (2 Kings 20:1-6)

Prayer - Day 15

A prayer of Daniel

3 And I set my face unto the Lord God, to seek by prayer and supplications, with fasting, and sackcloth, and ashes: 4 And I prayed unto the Lord my God, and made my confession, and said, O Lord, the great and dreadful God, keeping the covenant and mercy to them that love him, and to them that keep his commandments; 5 We have sinned, and have committed iniquity, and have done wickedly, and have rebelled, even by departing from thy precepts and from thy judgments: 6 Neither have we hearkened unto thy servants the prophets, which spake in thy name to our kings, our princes, and our fathers, and to all the people of the land. 7 O Lord, righteousness belongeth unto thee, but unto us confusion of faces, as at this day; to the men of Judah, and to the inhabitants of Jerusalem, and unto all Israel, that are near, and that are far off, through all the countries whither thou hast driven them, because of their trespass that they have trespassed against thee. 8 O Lord, to us belongeth confusion of face, to our kings, to our princes, and to our fathers, because we have sinned against thee. 9 To the Lord our God belong mercies and forgivenesses, though we have rebelled against him; 10 Neither have we obeyed the voice of the Lord our God, to walk in his laws, which he set before us by his servants the prophets.

3 And I prayed earnestly to the Lord God, pleading with him, fasting, wearing sackcloth, and sitting in ashes. 4 I prayed to the Lord my God and confessed the sins of my people. I said, "Lord God, you are great, and we honor you. You are faithful to your covenant and show constant love to those who love you and do what you command. 5 "We have sinned, we have been evil, we have done wrong. We have rejected what you commanded us to do and have turned away from what you showed us was right. 6 We have not listened to your servants the prophets, who spoke in your name to our kings, our rulers, our ancestors, and our whole nation. 7 You, Lord, always do what is right, but we have always brought disgrace on ourselves. This is true of all of us who live in Judea and in Jerusalem and of all the Israelites whom you scattered in countries near and far because they were unfaithful to you. 8 Our kings, our rulers, and our ancestors have acted shamefully and sinned against you, Lord. 9 You are merciful and forgiving, although we have rebelled against you. 10 We did not listen to you, O Lord our God, when you told us to live according to the laws which you gave us through your servants the prophets.

11 Yea, all Israel have transgressed thy law, even by departing, that they might not obey thy voice; therefore the curse is poured upon us, and the oath that is written in the law of Moses the servant of God, because we have sinned against him. 12 And he hath confirmed his words, which he spake against us, and against our judges that judged us, by bringing upon us a great evil: for under the whole heaven hath not been done as hath been done upon Jerusalem. 13 As it is written in the law of Moses, all this evil is come upon us: yet made we not our prayer before the Lord our God, that we might turn from our iniquities, and understand thy truth. 14 Therefore hath the Lord watched upon the evil, and brought it upon us: for the Lord our God is righteous in all his works which he doeth: for we obeyed not his voice. 15 And now, O Lord our God, that hast brought thy people forth out of the land of Egypt with a mighty hand, and hast gotten thee renown, as at this day; we have sinned, we have done wickedly. 16 O Lord, according to all thy righteousness, I beseech thee, let thine anger and thy fury be turned away from thy city Jerusalem, thy holy mountain: because for our sins, and for the iniquities of our fathers, Jerusalem and thy people are become a reproach to all that are about us. 17 Now therefore, O our God, hear the prayer of thy servant, and his supplications, and cause thy face to shine upon thy sanctuary that is desolate, for the Lord's sake.

11 All Israel broke your laws and refused to listen to what you said. We sinned against you, and so you brought on us the curses that are written in the Law of Moses, your servant. 12 You did what you said you would do to us and our rulers. You punished Jerusalem more severely than any other city on earth, 13 giving us all the punishment described in the Law of Moses. But even now, O Lord our God, we have not tried to please you by turning from our sins or by following your truth. 14 You, O Lord our God, were prepared to punish us, and you did, because you always do what is right, and we did not listen to you. 15 "O Lord our God, you showed your power by bringing your people out of Egypt, and your power is still remembered. We have sinned; we have done wrong. 16 You have defended us in the past, so do not be angry with Jerusalem any longer. It is your city, your sacred hill. All the people in the neighboring countries look down on Jerusalem and on your people because of our sins and the evil our ancestors did. 17 O God, hear my prayer and pleading. Restore your Temple, which has been destroyed; restore it so that everyone will know that you are God.

18 O my God, incline thine ear, and hear; open thine eyes, and behold our desolations, and the city which is called by thy name: for we do not present our supplications before thee for our righteousnesses, but for thy great mercies. 19 O Lord, hear; O Lord, forgive; O Lord, hearken and do; defer not, for thine own sake, O my God: for thy city and thy people are called by thy name. 20 And whiles I was speaking, and praying, and confessing my sin and the sin of my people Israel, and presenting my supplication before the Lord my God for the holy mountain of my God; 21 Yea, whiles I was speaking in prayer, even the man Gabriel, whom I had seen in the vision at the beginning, being caused to fly swiftly, touched me about the time of the evening oblation. 22 And he informed me, and talked with me, and said, O Daniel, I am now come forth to give thee skill and understanding. 23 At the beginning of thy supplications the commandment came forth, and I am come to shew thee; for thou art greatly beloved: therefore understand the matter, and consider the vision. 24 Seventy weeks are determined upon thy people and upon thy holy city, to finish the transgression, and to make an end of sins, and to make reconciliation for iniquity, and to bring in everlasting righteousness, and to seal up the vision and prophecy, and to anoint the most Holy.

18 Listen to us, O God; look at us and see the trouble we are in and the suffering of the city that bears your name. We are praying to you because you are merciful, not because we have done right. 19 Lord, hear us. Lord, forgive us. Lord, listen to us, and act! In order that everyone will know that you are God, do not delay! This city and these people are yours." 20 I went on praying, confessing my sins and the sins of my people Israel and pleading with the Lord my God to restore his holy Temple. 21 While I was praying, Gabriel, whom I had seen in the earlier vision, came flying down to where I was. It was the time for the evening sacrifice to be offered. 22 He explained, "Daniel, I have come here to help you understand the prophecy. 23 When you began to plead with God, he answered you. He loves you, and so I have come to tell you the answer. Now pay attention while I explain the vision. 24 "Seven times seventy years is the length of time God has set for freeing your people and your holy city from sin and evil. Sin will be forgiven and eternal justice established, so that the vision and the prophecy will come true, and the holy Temple will be rededicated.

25 Know therefore and understand, that from the going forth of the commandment to restore and to build Jerusalem unto the Messiah the Prince shall be seven weeks, and threescore and two weeks: the street shall be built again, and the wall, even in troublous times. 26 And after threescore and two weeks shall Messiah be cut off, but not for himself: and the people of the prince that shall come shall destroy the city and the sanctuary; and the end thereof shall be with a flood, and unto the end of the war desolations are determined. 27 And he shall confirm the covenant with many for one week: and in the midst of the week he shall cause the sacrifice and the oblation to cease, and for the overspreading of abominations he shall make it desolate, even until the consummation, and that determined shall be poured upon the desolate. (Daniel 9:3-27)

25 Note this and understand it: From the time the command is given to rebuild Jerusalem until God's chosen leader, the messiah comes, seven times seven years will pass. Jerusalem will be rebuilt with streets and strong defenses, and will stand for seven times sixty-two years, but this will be a time of troubles. 26 And at the end of that time God's chosen leader, the Messiah will be killed unjustly. The city and the Temple will be destroyed by the invading army of a powerful ruler. The end will come like a flood, bringing the war and destruction which God has prepared. 27 That ruler will have a firm agreement with many people for seven years, and when half this time is past, he will put an end to sacrifices and offerings. The Awful Horror will be placed on the highest point of the Temple and will remain there until the one who put it there meets the end which God has prepared for him." (Daniel 9:3-27)

Prayer - Day 16

A prayer of Solomon

22 And Solomon stood before the altar of the Lord in the presence of all the congregation of Israel, and spread forth his hands toward heaven: 23 And he said, Lord God of Israel, there is no God like thee, in heaven above, or on earth beneath, who keepest covenant and mercy with thy servants that walk before thee with all their heart: 24 Who hast kept with thy servant David my father that thou promisedst him: thou spakest also with thy mouth, and hast fulfilled it with thine hand, as it is this day. 25 Therefore now, Lord God of Israel, keep with thy servant David my father that thou promisedst him, saying, There shall not fail thee a man in my sight to sit on the throne of Israel; so that thy children take heed to their way, that they walk before me as thou hast walked before me. 26 And now, O God of Israel, let thy word, I pray thee, be verified, which thou spakest unto thy servant David my father. 27 But will God indeed dwell on the earth? behold, the heaven and heaven of heavens cannot contain thee; how much less this house that I have builded? 28 Yet have thou respect unto the prayer of thy servant, and to his supplication, O Lord my God, to hearken unto the cry and to the prayer, which thy servant prayeth before thee to day:

22 Then in the presence of the people Solomon went and stood in front of the altar of the Lord, where he raised his arms 23 and prayed, "Lord God of Israel, there is no god like you in heaven above or on earth below! You keep your covenant with your people and show them your love when they live in wholehearted obedience to you. 24 You have kept the promise you made to my father David; today every word has been fulfilled. 25 And now, Lord God of Israel, I pray that you will also keep the other promise you made to my father when you told him that there would always be one of his descendants ruling as king of Israel, provided they obeyed you as carefully as he did. 26 So now, O God of Israel, let everything come true that you promised to my father David, your servant. 27 "But can you, O God, really live on earth? Not even all of heaven is large enough to hold you, so how can this Temple that I have built be large enough? 28 Lord my God, I am your servant. Listen to my prayer, and grant the requests I make to you today.

29 That thine eyes may be open toward this house night and day, even toward the place of which thou hast said, My name shall be there: that thou mayest hearken unto the prayer which thy servant shall make toward this place. 30 And hearken thou to the supplication of thy servant, and of thy people Israel, when they shall pray toward this place: and hear thou in heaven thy dwelling place: and when thou hearest, forgive. 31 If any man trespass against his neighbour, and an oath be laid upon him to cause him to swear, and the oath come before thine altar in this house: 32 Then hear thou in heaven, and do, and judge thy servants, condemning the wicked, to bring his way upon his head; and justifying the righteous, to give him according to his righteousness. 33 When thy people Israel be smitten down before the enemy, because they have sinned against thee, and shall turn again to thee, and confess thy name, and pray, and make supplication unto thee in this house: 34 Then hear thou in heaven, and forgive the sin of thy people Israel, and bring them again unto the land which thou gavest unto their fathers. 35 When heaven is shut up, and there is no rain, because they have sinned against thee; if they pray toward this place, and confess thy name, and turn from their sin, when thou afflictest them: 36 Then hear thou in heaven, and forgive the sin of thy servants, and of thy people Israel, that thou teach them the good way wherein they should walk, and give rain upon thy land, which thou hast given to thy people for an inheritance.

29 Watch over this Temple day and night, this place where you have chosen to be worshiped. Hear me when I face this Temple and pray. 30 Hear my prayers and the prayers of your people when they face this place and pray. In your home in heaven hear us and forgive us. 31 "When a person is accused of wronging another and is brought to your altar in this Temple to take an oath that he is innocent, 32 O Lord, listen in heaven and judge your servants. Punish the guilty one as he deserves, and acquit the one who is innocent. 33 "When your people Israel are defeated by their enemies because they have sinned against you, and then when they turn to you and come to this Temple, humbly praying to you for forgiveness, 34 listen to them in heaven. Forgive the sins of your people and bring them back to the land which you gave to their ancestors. 35 "When you hold back the rain because your people have sinned against you, and then when they repent and face this Temple, humbly praying to you, 36 listen to them in heaven. Forgive the sins of the king and of the people of Israel, and teach them to do what is right. Then, O Lord, send rain on this land of yours, which you gave to your people as a permanent possession.

37 If there be in the land famine, if there be pestilence, blasting, mildew, locust, or if there be caterpiller; if their enemy besiege them in the land of their cities; whatsoever plague, whatsoever sickness there be; 38 What prayer and supplication soever be made by any man, or by all thy people Israel, which shall know every man the plague of his own heart, and spread forth his hands toward this house: 39 Then hear thou in heaven thy dwelling place, and forgive, and do, and give to every man according to his ways, whose heart thou knowest; (for thou, even thou only, knowest the hearts of all the children of men;) 40 That they may fear thee all the days that they live in the land which thou gavest unto our fathers. 41 Moreover concerning a stranger, that is not of thy people Israel, but cometh out of a far country for thy name's sake; 42 (For they shall hear of thy great name, and of thy strong hand, and of thy stretched out arm;) when he shall come and pray toward this house; 43 Hear thou in heaven thy dwelling place, and do according to all that the stranger calleth to thee for: that all people of the earth may know thy name, to fear thee, as do thy people Israel; and that they may know that this house, which I have builded, is called by thy name. 44 If thy people go out to battle against their enemy, whithersoever thou shalt send them, and shall pray unto the Lord toward the city which thou hast chosen, and toward the house that I have built for thy name: 45 Then hear thou in heaven their prayer and their supplication, and maintain their cause.

37 "When there is famine in the land or an epidemic or the crops are destroyed by scorching winds or swarms of locusts, or when your people are attacked by their enemies, or when there is disease or sickness among them, 38 listen to their prayers. If any of your people Israel, out of heartfelt sorrow, stretch out their hands in prayer toward this Temple, 39 hear their prayer. Listen to them in your home in heaven, forgive them, and help them. You alone know the thoughts of the human heart. Deal with each person as he deserves, 40 so that your people may obey you all the time they live in the land which you gave to our ancestors. 41-42 "When a foreigner who lives in a distant land hears of your fame and of the great things you have done for your people and comes to worship you and to pray at this Temple, 43 listen to his prayer. In heaven, where you live, hear him and do what he asks you to do, so that all the peoples of the world may know you and obey you, as your people Israel do. Then they will know that this Temple I have built is the place where you are to be worshiped. 44 "When you command your people to go into battle against their enemies and they pray to you, wherever they are, facing this city which you have chosen and this Temple which I have built for you, 45 listen to their prayers. Hear them in heaven and give them victory.

46 If they sin against thee, (for there is no man that sinneth not,) and thou be angry with them, and deliver them to the enemy, so that they carry them away captives unto the land of the enemy, far or near; 47 Yet if they shall bethink themselves in the land whither they were carried captives, and repent, and make supplication unto thee in the land of them that carried them captives, saying, We have sinned, and have done perversely, we have committed wickedness; 48 And so return unto thee with all their heart, and with all their soul, in the land of their enemies, which led them away captive, and pray unto thee toward their land, which thou gavest unto their fathers, the city which thou hast chosen, and the house which I have built for thy name: 49 Then hear thou their prayer and their supplication in heaven thy dwelling place, and maintain their cause, 50 And forgive thy people that have sinned against thee, and all their transgressions wherein they have transgressed against thee, and give them compassion before them who carried them captive, that they may have compassion on them: 51 For they be thy people, and thine inheritance, which thou broughtest forth out of Egypt, from the midst of the furnace of iron: 52 That thine eyes may be open unto the supplication of thy servant, and unto the supplication of thy people Israel, to hearken unto them in all that they call for unto thee. O Lord God.

46 "When your people sin against you—and there is no one who does not sin—and in your anger you let their enemies defeat them and take them as prisoners to some other land, even if that land is far away, 47 listen to your people's prayers. If there in that land they repent and pray to you, confessing how sinful and wicked they have been, hear their prayers, O Lord. 48 If in that land they truly and sincerely repent and pray to you as they face toward this land which you gave to our ancestors, this city which you have chosen, and this Temple which I have built for you, 49 then listen to their prayers. In your home in heaven hear them and be merciful to them. 50 Forgive all their sins and their rebellion against you, and make their enemies treat them with kindness. 51 They are your own people, whom you brought out of Egypt, that blazing furnace. 52 "Sovereign Lord, may you always look with favor on your people Israel and their king, and hear their prayer whenever they call to you for help.

53 For thou didst separate them from among all the people of the earth, to be thine inheritance, as thou spakest by the hand of Moses thy servant, when thou broughtest our fathers out of Egypt, 54 And it was so, that when Solomon had made an end of praying all this prayer and supplication unto the Lord, he arose from before the altar of the Lord, from kneeling on his knees with his hands spread up to heaven.. (1 Kings 8:22-54)

53 You chose them from all the peoples to be your own people, as you told them through your servant Moses when you brought our ancestors out of Egypt." 54 After Solomon had finished praying to the Lord, he stood up in front of the altar, where he had been kneeling with uplifted hands. (1 Kings 8:22-54)

Prayer - Day 17

The Israelites prayer of confession

1 Now in the twenty and fourth day of this month the children of Israel were assembled with fasting, and with sackclothes, and earth upon them. 2 And the seed of Israel separated themselves from all strangers, and stood and confessed their sins, and the iniquities of their fathers. 3 And they stood up in their place, and read in the book of the law of the Lord their God one fourth part of the day; and another fourth part they confessed, and worshipped the Lord their God. 4 Then stood up upon the stairs, of the Levites, Jeshua, and Bani, Kadmiel, Shebaniah, Bunni, Sherebiah, Bani, and Chenani, and cried with a loud voice unto the Lord their God. 5 Then the Levites, Jeshua, and Kadmiel, Bani, Hashabniah, Sherebiah, Hodijah, Shebaniah, and Pethahiah, said, Stand up and bless the Lord your God for ever and ever: and blessed be thy glorious name, which is exalted above all blessing and praise. 6 Thou, even thou, art Lord alone; thou hast made heaven, the heaven of heavens, with all their host, the earth, and all things that are therein, the seas, and all that is therein, and thou preservest them all; and the host of heaven worshippeth thee. 7 Thou art the Lord the God, who didst choose Abram, and broughtest him forth out of Ur of the Chaldees, and gavest him the name of Abraham;

1-2 On the twenty-fourth day of the same month the people of Israel gathered to fast in order to show sorrow for their sins. They had already separated themselves from all foreigners. They wore sackcloth and put dust on their heads as signs of grief. Then they stood and began to confess the sins that they and their ancestors had committed. 3 For about three hours the Law of the Lord their God was read to them, and for the next three hours they confessed their sins and worshiped the Lord their God. 4 There was a platform for the Levites, and on it stood Jeshua, Bani, Kadmiel, Shebaniah, Bunni, Sherebiah, Bani, and Chenani. They prayed aloud to the Lord their God. 5 The following Levites gave a call to worship: Jeshua, Kadmiel, Bani, Hashabneiah, Sherebiah, Hodiah, Shebaniah, and Pethahiah. They said: "Stand up and praise the Lord your God; praise him forever and ever! Let everyone praise his glorious name, although no human praise is great enough." 6 And then the people of Israel prayed this prayer: "You, Lord, you alone are Lord; you made the heavens and the stars of the sky. You made land and sea and everything in them; you gave life to all. The heavenly powers bow down and worship you. 7 You, Lord God, chose Abram and led him out of Ur in Babylonia; you changed his name to Abraham.

8 And foundest his heart faithful before thee, and madest a covenant with him to give the land of the Canaanites, the Hittites, the Amorites, and the Perizzites, and the Jebusites, and the Girgashites, to give it, I say, to his seed, and hast performed thy words; for thou art righteous: 9 And didst see the affliction of our fathers in Egypt, and heardest their cry by the Red sea; 10 And shewedst signs and wonders upon Pharaoh, and on all his servants, and on all the people of his land: for thou knewest that they dealt proudly against them. So didst thou get thee a name, as it is this day. 11 And thou didst divide the sea before them, so that they went through the midst of the sea on the dry land; and their persecutors thou threwest into the deeps, as a stone into the mighty waters. 12 Moreover thou leddest them in the day by a cloudy pillar; and in the night by a pillar of fire, to give them light in the way wherein they should go. 13 Thou camest down also upon mount Sinai, and spakest with them from heaven, and gavest them right judgments, and true laws, good statutes and commandments: 14 And madest known unto them thy holy sabbath, and commandedst them precepts, statutes, and laws, by the hand of Moses thy servant: 15 And gavest them bread from heaven for their hunger, and broughtest forth water for them out of the rock for their thirst, and promisedst them that they should go in to possess the land which thou hadst sworn to give them. 16 But they and our fathers dealt proudly, and hardened their necks, and hearkened not to thy commandments,

8 You found that he was faithful to you, and you made a covenant with him. You promised to give him the land of the Canaanites, the land of the Hittites and the Amorites, the land of the Perizzites, the Jebusites, the Girgashites, to be a land where his descendants would live. You kept your promise, because you are faithful. 9 "You saw how our ancestors suffered in Egypt; you heard their call for help at the Red Sea. 10 You worked amazing miracles against the king, against his officials and the people of his land, because you knew how they oppressed your people. You won then the fame you still have today. 11 Through the sea you made a path for your people and led them through on dry ground. Those who pursued them drowned in deep water, as a stone sinks in the raging sea. 12 With a cloud you led them in daytime, and at night you lighted their way with fire. 13 At Mount Sinai you came down from heaven; you spoke to your people and gave them good laws and sound teachings. 14 You taught them to keep your Sabbaths holy, and through your servant Moses you gave them your laws. 15 "When they were hungry, you gave them bread from heaven, and water from a rock when they were thirsty. You told them to take control of the land which you had promised to give them. 16 But our ancestors grew proud and stubborn and refused to obey your commands.

17 And refused to obey, neither were mindful of thy wonders that thou didst among them; but hardened their necks, and in their rebellion appointed a captain to return to their bondage: but thou art a God ready to pardon, gracious and merciful, slow to anger, and of great kindness, and forsookest them not. 18 Yea, when they had made them a molten calf, and said, This is thy God that brought thee up out of Egypt, and had wrought great provocations; 19 Yet thou in thy manifold mercies forsookest them not in the wilderness: the pillar of the cloud departed not from them by day, to lead them in the way; neither the pillar of fire by night, to shew them light, and the way wherein they should go. 20 Thou gavest also thy good spirit to instruct them, and withheldest not thy manna from their mouth, and gavest them water for their thirst. 21 Yea, forty years didst thou sustain them in the wilderness, so that they lacked nothing; their clothes waxed not old, and their feet swelled not. 22 Moreover thou gavest them kingdoms and nations, and didst divide them into corners: so they possessed the land of Sihon, and the land of the king of Heshbon, and the land of Og king of Bashan. 23 Their children also multipliedst thou as the stars of heaven, and broughtest them into the land, concerning which thou hadst promised to their fathers, that they should go in to possess it.

17 They refused to obey; they forgot all you did; they forgot the miracles you had performed. In their pride they chose a leader to take them back to slavery in Egypt. But you are a God who forgives; you are gracious and loving, slow to be angry. Your mercy is great; you did not forsake them. 18 They made an idol in the shape of a bull-calf and said it was the god who led them from Egypt! How much they insulted you, Lord! 19 But you did not abandon them there in the desert, for your mercy is great. You did not take away the cloud or the fire that showed them the path by day and night. 20 In your goodness you told them what they should do; you fed them manna and gave them water to drink. 21 Through forty years in the desert you provided all that they needed; their clothing never wore out, and their feet were not swollen with pain. 22 "You let them conquer nations and kingdoms, lands that bordered their own. They conquered the land of Heshbon, where Sihon ruled, and the land of Bashan, where Og was king. 23 You gave them as many children as there are stars in the sky, and let them conquer and live in the land that you had promised their ancestors to give them.

24 So the children went in and possessed the land, and thou subduedst before them the inhabitants of the land, the Canaanites, and gavest them into their hands, with their kings, and the people of the land, that they might do with them as they would. 25 And they took strong cities, and a fat land, and possessed houses full of all goods, wells digged, vineyards, and oliveyards, and fruit trees in abundance: so they did eat, and were filled, and became fat, and delighted themselves in thy great goodness. 26 Nevertheless they were disobedient, and rebelled against thee, and cast thy law behind their backs, and slew thy prophets which testified against them to turn them to thee, and they wrought great provocations. 27 Therefore thou deliveredst them into the hand of their enemies, who vexed them: and in the time of their trouble, when they cried unto thee, thou heardest them from heaven; and according to thy manifold mercies thou gavest them saviours, who saved them out of the hand of their enemies. 28 But after they had rest, they did evil again before thee: therefore leftest thou them in the land of their enemies, so that they had the dominion over them: yet when they returned, and cried unto thee, thou heardest them from heaven; and many times didst thou deliver them according to thy mercies; 29 And testifiedst against them, that thou mightest bring them again unto thy law: yet they dealt proudly, and hearkened not unto thy commandments, but sinned against thy judgments, (which if a man do, he shall live in them;) and withdrew the shoulder, and hardened their neck, and would not hear.

24 They conquered the land of Canaan; you overcame the people living there. You gave your people the power to do as they pleased with the people and kings of Canaan. 25 Your people captured fortified cities, fertile land, houses full of wealth, cisterns already dug, olive trees, fruit trees, and vineyards. They ate all they wanted and grew fat; they enjoyed all the good things you gave them. 26 "But your people rebelled and disobeyed you; they turned their backs on your Law. They killed the prophets who warned them, who told them to turn back to you. They insulted you time after time, 27 so you let their enemies conquer and rule them. In their trouble they called to you for help, and you answered them from heaven. In your great mercy you sent them leaders who rescued them from their foes. 28 When peace returned, they sinned again, and again you let their enemies conquer them. Yet when they repented and asked you to save them, in heaven you heard, and time after time you rescued them in your great mercy. 29 You warned them to obey your teachings, but in pride they rejected your laws, although keeping your Law is the way to life. Hard-headed and stubborn, they refused to obey.

30 Yet many years didst thou forbear them, and testifiedst against them by thy spirit in thy prophets: yet would they not give ear: therefore gavest thou them into the hand of the people of the lands. 31 Nevertheless for thy great mercies' sake thou didst not utterly consume them, nor forsake them; for thou art a gracious and merciful God. 32 Now therefore, our God, the great, the mighty, and the terrible God, who keepest covenant and mercy, let not all the trouble seem little before thee, that hath come upon us, on our kings, on our princes, and on our priests, and on our prophets, and on our fathers, and on all thy people, since the time of the kings of Assyria unto this day. 33 Howbeit thou art just in all that is brought upon us; for thou hast done right, but we have done wickedly: 34 Neither have our kings, our princes, our priests, nor our fathers, kept thy law, nor hearkened unto thy commandments and thy testimonies, wherewith thou didst testify against them. 35 For they have not served thee in their kingdom, and in thy great goodness that thou gavest them, and in the large and fat land which thou gavest before them, neither turned they from their wicked works. 36 Behold, we are servants this day, and for the land that thou gavest unto our fathers to eat the fruit thereof and the good thereof, behold, we are servants in it: 37 And it yieldeth much increase unto the kings whom thou hast set over us because of our sins: also they have dominion over our bodies, and over our cattle, at their pleasure, and we are in great distress.

30 Year after year you patiently warned them. You inspired your prophets to speak, but your people were deaf, so you let them be conquered by other nations. 31 And yet, because your mercy is great, you did not forsake or destroy them.
You are a gracious and merciful God! 32 "O God, our God, how great you are! How terrifying, how powerful! You faithfully keep your covenant promises. From the time when Assyrian kings oppressed us, even till now, how much we have suffered! Our kings, our leaders, our priests and prophets, our ancestors, and all our people have suffered.
Remember how much we have suffered! 33 You have done right to punish us; you have been faithful, even though we have sinned. 34 Our ancestors, our kings, leaders, and priests have not kept your Law. They did not listen to your commands and warnings. 35 With your blessing, kings ruled your people when they lived in the broad, fertile land you gave them; but they failed to turn from sin and serve you. 36 And now we are slaves in the land that you gave us, this fertile land which gives us food. 37 What the land produces goes to the kings that you put over us because we sinned. They do as they please with us and our livestock, and we are in deep distress!"

38 And because of all this we make a sure covenant, and write it; and our princes, Levites, and priests, seal unto it. (Nehemiah 9:1-38)

38 Because of all that has happened, we, the people of Israel, hereby make a solemn written agreement, and our leaders, our Levites, and our priests put their seals to it. (Nehemiah 9:1-38)

Prayer - Day 18

A prayer of Jesus

36 Then cometh Jesus with them unto a place called Gethsemane, and saith unto the disciples, Sit ye here, while I go and pray yonder. 37 And he took with him Peter and the two sons of Zebedee, and began to be sorrowful and very heavy. 38 Then saith he unto them, My soul is exceeding sorrowful, even unto death: tarry ye here, and watch with me. 39 And he went a little farther, and fell on his face, and prayed, saying, O my Father, if it be possible, let this cup pass from me: nevertheless not as I will, but as thou wilt. 40 And he cometh unto the disciples, and findeth them asleep, and saith unto Peter, What, could ye not watch with me one hour? 41 Watch and pray, that ye enter not into temptation: the spirit indeed is willing, but the flesh is weak. 42 He went away again the second time, and prayed, saying, O my Father, if this cup may not pass away from me, except I drink it, thy will be done. 43 And he came and found them asleep again: for their eyes were heavy. 44 And he left them, and went away again, and prayed the third time, saying the same words. (Matthew 26:36-44)

36 Then Jesus went with his disciples to a place called Gethsemane, and he said to them, "Sit here while I go over there and pray." 37 He took with him Peter and the two sons of Zebedee. Grief and anguish came over him, 38 and he said to them, "The sorrow in my heart is so great that it almost crushes me. Stay here and keep watch with me." 39 He went a little farther on, threw himself face downward on the ground, and prayed, "My Father, if it is possible, take this cup of suffering from me! Yet not what I want, but what you want." 40 Then he returned to the three disciples and found them asleep; and he said to Peter, "How is it that you three were not able to keep watch with me for even one hour? 41 Keep watch and pray that you will not fall into temptation. The spirit is willing, but the flesh is weak." 42 Once more Jesus went away and prayed, "My Father, if this cup of suffering cannot be taken away unless I drink it, your will be done." 43 He returned once more and found the disciples asleep; they could not keep their eyes open. 44 Again Jesus left them, went away, and prayed the third time, saying the same words. (Matthew 26:36-44)

A prayer of Jonah

1 Then Jonah prayed unto the Lord his God out of the fish's belly, 2 And said, I cried by reason of mine affliction unto the Lord, and he heard me; out of the belly of hell cried I, and thou heardest my voice. 3 For thou hadst cast me into the deep, in the midst of the seas; and the floods compassed me about: all thy billows and thy waves passed over me. 4 Then I said, I am cast out of thy sight; yet I will look again toward thy holy temple. 5 The waters compassed me about, even to the soul: the depth closed me round about, the weeds were wrapped about my head. 6 I went down to the bottoms of the mountains; the earth with her bars was about me for ever: yet hast thou brought up my life from corruption, O Lord my God. 7 When my soul fainted within me I remembered the Lord: and my prayer came in unto thee, into thine holy temple. 8 They that observe lying vanities forsake their own mercy. 9 But I will sacrifice unto thee with the voice of thanksgiving; I will pay that that I have vowed. Salvation is of the Lord. 10 And the Lord spake unto the fish, and it vomited out Jonah upon the dry land.

(Jonah 2:1-10)

1 From deep inside the fish Jonah prayed to the Lord his God: 2 "In my distress, O Lord, I called to you, and you answered me. from deep in the world of the dead I cried for help, and you heard me. 3 You threw me down into the depths, to the very bottom of the sea, where the waters were all around me, and all your mighty waves rolled over me.
4 I thought I had been banished from your presence and would never see your holy Temple again. 5 The water came over me and choked me; the sea covered me completely, and seaweed wrapped around my head. 6 I went down to the very roots of the mountains, into the land whose gates lock shut forever. But you, O Lord my God, brought me back from the depths alive. 7 When I felt my life slipping away, then, O Lord, I prayed to you, and in your holy Temple you heard me. 8 Those who worship worthless idols have abandoned their loyalty to you. 9 But I will sing praises to you; I will offer you a sacrifice and do what I have promised. Salvation comes from the Lord!" 10 Then the Lord ordered the fish to spit Jonah up on the beach, and it did.

(Jonah 2:1-10)

Prayer - Day 19

Prayer of the self-righteous verses the humble prayer

9 And he spake this parable unto certain which trusted in themselves that they were righteous, and despised others: 10 Two men went up into the temple to pray; the one a Pharisee, and the other a publican. 11 The Pharisee stood and prayed thus with himself, God, I thank thee, that I am not as other men are, extortioners, unjust, adulterers, or even as this publican. 12 I fast twice in the week, I give tithes of all that I possess. 13 And the publican, standing afar off, would not lift up so much as his eyes unto heaven, but smote upon his breast, saying, God be merciful to me a sinner. 14 I tell you, this man went down to his house justified rather than the other: for every one that exalteth himself shall be abased; and he that humbleth himself shall be exalted. (Luke 18:9-14)

9 Jesus also told this parable to people who were sure of their own goodness and despised everybody else. 10 "Once there were two men who went up to the Temple to pray: one was a Pharisee, the other a tax collector. 11 The Pharisee stood apart by himself and prayed, 'I thank you, God, that I am not greedy, dishonest, or an adulterer, like everybody else. I thank you that I am not like that tax collector over there. 12 I fast two days a week, and I give you one tenth of all my income.' 13 But the tax collector stood at a distance and would not even raise his face to heaven, but beat on his breast and said, 'God, have pity on me, a sinner!' 14 I tell you," said Jesus, "the tax collector, and not the Pharisee, was in the right with God when he went home. For those who make themselves great will be humbled, and those who humble themselves will be made great." . (Luke 18:9-14)

A prayer psalm of David

1 Save me, O God; for the waters are come in unto my soul. 2 I sink in deep mire, where there is no standing: I am come into deep waters, where the floods overflow me. 3 I am weary of my crying: my throat is dried: mine eyes fail while I wait for my God.

1 Save me, O God! The water is up to my neck; 2 I am sinking in deep mud, and there is no solid ground;
I am out in deep water, and the waves are about to drown me. 3 I am worn out from calling for help, and my throat is aching. I have strained my eyes, looking for your help.

4 They that hate me without a cause are more than the hairs of mine head: they that would destroy me, being mine enemies wrongfully, are mighty: then I restored that which I took not away. 5 O God, thou knowest my foolishness; and my sins are not hid from thee. 6 Let not them that wait on thee, O Lord God of hosts, be ashamed for my sake: let not those that seek thee be confounded for my sake, O God of Israel. 7 Because for thy sake I have borne reproach; shame hath covered my face. 8 I am become a stranger unto my brethren, and an alien unto my mother's children. 9 For the zeal of thine house hath eaten me up; and the reproaches of them that reproached thee are fallen upon me. 10 When I wept, and chastened my soul with fasting, that was to my reproach. 11 I made sackcloth also my garment; and I became a proverb to them. 12 They that sit in the gate speak against me; and I was the song of the drunkards. 13 But as for me, my prayer is unto thee, O Lord, in an acceptable time: O God, in the multitude of thy mercy hear me, in the truth of thy salvation. 14 Deliver me out of the mire, and let me not sink: let me be delivered from them that hate me, and out of the deep waters. 15 Let not the waterflood overflow me, neither let the deep swallow me up, and let not the pit shut her mouth upon me. 16 Hear me, O Lord; for thy lovingkindness is good: turn unto me according to the multitude of thy tender mercies. 17 And hide not thy face from thy servant; for I am in trouble: hear me speedily. 18 Draw nigh unto my soul, and redeem it: deliver me because of mine enemies.

4 Those who hate me for no reason are more numerous than the hairs of my head. My enemies tell lies against me; they are strong and want to kill me. They made me give back things I did not steal. 5 My sins, O God, are not hidden from you; you know how foolish I have been. 6 Don't let me bring shame on those who trust in you, Sovereign Lord Almighty! Don't let me bring disgrace to those who worship you, O God of Israel! 7 It is for your sake that I have been insulted and that I am covered with shame. 8 I am like a stranger to my relatives, like a foreigner to my family. 9 My devotion to your Temple burns in me like a fire; the insults which are hurled at you fall on me.
10 I humble myself by fasting, and people insult me; 11 I dress myself in clothes of mourning, and they laugh at me. 12 They talk about me in the streets, and drunkards make up songs about me. 13 But as for me, I will pray to you, Lord; answer me, God, at a time you choose. Answer me because of your great love, because you keep your promise to save.
14 Save me from sinking in the mud; keep me safe from my enemies, safe from the deep water. 15 Don't let the flood come over me; don't let me drown in the depths or sink into the grave. 16 Answer me, Lord, in the goodness of your constant love; in your great compassion turn to me! 17 Don't hide yourself from your servant; I am in great trouble—answer me now! 18 Come to me and save me; rescue me from my enemies.

19 Thou hast known my reproach, and my shame, and my dishonour: mine adversaries are all before thee. 20 Reproach hath broken my heart; and I am full of heaviness: and I looked for some to take pity, but there was none; and for comforters, but I found none. 21 They gave me also gall for my meat; and in my thirst they gave me vinegar to drink. 22 Let their table become a snare before them: and that which should have been for their welfare, let it become a trap. 23 Let their eyes be darkened, that they see not; and make their loins continually to shake. 24 Pour out thine indignation upon them, and let thy wrathful anger take hold of them. 25 Let their habitation be desolate; and let none dwell in their tents. 26 For they persecute him whom thou hast smitten; and they talk to the grief of those whom thou hast wounded. 27 Add iniquity unto their iniquity: and let them not come into thy righteousness. 28 Let them be blotted out of the book of the living, and not be written with the righteous. 29 But I am poor and sorrowful: let thy salvation, O God, set me up on high. (Psalms 69:1-29)

19 You know how I am insulted, how I am disgraced and dishonored; you see all my enemies. 20 Insults have broken my heart, and I am in despair. I had hoped for sympathy, but there was none; for comfort, but I found none. 21 When I was hungry, they gave me poison; when I was thirsty, they offered me vinegar. 22 May their banquets cause their ruin; may their sacred feasts cause their downfall. 23 Strike them with blindness! Make their backs always weak! 24 Pour out your anger on them; let your indignation overtake them. 25 May their camps be left deserted; may no one be left alive in their tents. 26 They persecute those whom you have punished; they talk about the sufferings of those you have wounded. 27 Keep a record of all their sins; don't let them have any part in your salvation. 28 May their names be erased from the book of the living; may they not be included in the list of your people. 29 But I am in pain and despair; lift me up, O God, and save me!. (Psalms 69:1-29)

Prayer - Day 20

A prayer of Jesus

1 These words spake Jesus, and lifted up his eyes to heaven, and said, Father, the hour is come; glorify thy Son, that thy Son also may glorify thee: 2 As thou hast given him power over all flesh, that he should give eternal life to as many as thou hast given him. 3 And this is life eternal, that they might know thee the only true God, and Jesus Christ, whom thou hast sent. 4 I have glorified thee on the earth: I have finished the work which thou gavest me to do. 5 And now, O Father, glorify thou me with thine own self with the glory which I had with thee before the world was. 6 I have manifested thy name unto the men which thou gavest me out of the world: thine they were, and thou gavest them me; and they have kept thy word. 7 Now they have known that all things whatsoever thou hast given me are of thee. 8 For I have given unto them the words which thou gavest me; and they have received them, and have known surely that I came out from thee, and they have believed that thou didst send me. 9 I pray for them: I pray not for the world, but for them which thou hast given me; for they are thine. 10 And all mine are thine, and thine are mine; and I am glorified in them. 11 And now I am no more in the world, but these are in the world, and I come to thee. Holy Father, keep through thine own name those whom thou hast given me, that they may be one, as we are.

1 After Jesus finished saying this, he looked up to heaven and said, "Father, the hour has come. Give glory to your Son, so that the Son may give glory to you. 2 For you gave him authority over all people, so that he might give eternal life to all those you gave him. 3 And eternal life means to know you, the only true God, and to know Jesus Christ, whom you sent. 4 I have shown your glory on earth; I have finished the work you gave me to do. 5 Father! Give me glory in your presence now, the same glory I had with you before the world was made. 6 "I have made you known to those you gave me out of the world. They belonged to you, and you gave them to me. They have obeyed your word, 7 and now they know that everything you gave me comes from you. 8 I gave them the message that you gave me, and they received it; they know that it is true that I came from you, and they believe that you sent me. 9 "I pray for them. I do not pray for the world but for those you gave me, for they belong to you. 10 All I have is yours, and all you have is mine; and my glory is shown through them. 11 And now I am coming to you; I am no longer in the world, but they are in the world. Holy Father! Keep them safe by the power of your name, the name you gave me, so that they may be one just as you and I are one.

12 While I was with them in the world, I kept them in thy name: those that thou gavest me I have kept, and none of them is lost, but the son of perdition; that the scripture might be fulfilled. 13 And now come I to thee; and these things I speak in the world, that they might have my joy fulfilled in themselves. 14 I have given them thy word; and the world hath hated them, because they are not of the world, even as I am not of the world. 15 I pray not that thou shouldest take them out of the world, but that thou shouldest keep them from the evil. 16 They are not of the world, even as I am not of the world. 17 Sanctify them through thy truth: thy word is truth. 18 As thou hast sent me into the world, even so have I also sent them into the world. 19 And for their sakes I sanctify myself, that they also might be sanctified through the truth. 20 Neither pray I for these alone, but for them also which shall believe on me through their word; 21 That they all may be one; as thou, Father, art in me, and I in thee, that they also may be one in us: that the world may believe that thou hast sent me. 22 And the glory which thou gavest me I have given them; that they may be one, even as we are one: 23 I in them, and thou in me, that they may be made perfect in one; and that the world may know that thou hast sent me, and hast loved them, as thou hast loved me. 24 Father, I will that they also, whom thou hast given me, be with me where I am; that they may behold my glory, which thou hast given me: for thou lovedst me before the foundation of the world.

12 While I was with them, I kept them safe by the power of your name, the name you gave me. I protected them, and not one of them was lost, except the man who was bound to be lost—so that the scripture might come true. 13 And now I am coming to you, and I say these things in the world so that they might have my joy in their hearts in all its fullness. 14 I gave them your message, and the world hated them, because they do not belong to the world, just as I do not belong to the world. 15 I do not ask you to take them out of the world, but I do ask you to keep them safe from the Evil One. 16 Just as I do not belong to the world, they do not belong to the world. 17 Dedicate them to yourself by means of the truth; your word is truth. 18 I sent them into the world, just as you sent me into the world. 19 And for their sake I dedicate myself to you, in order that they, too, may be truly dedicated to you. 20 "I pray not only for them, but also for those who believe in me because of their message. 21 I pray that they may all be one. Father! May they be in us, just as you are in me and I am in you. May they be one, so that the world will believe that you sent me. 22 I gave them the same glory you gave me, so that they may be one, just as you and I are one: 23 I in them and you in me, so that they may be completely one, in order that the world may know that you sent me and that you love them as you love me. 24 "Father! You have given them to me, and I want them to be with me where I am, so that they may see my glory, the glory you gave me; for you loved me before the world was made.

25 O righteous Father, the world hath not known thee: but I have known thee, and these have known that thou hast sent me. 26 And I have declared unto them thy name, and will declare it: that the love wherewith thou hast loved me may be in them, and I in them. . (John 17:1-26)

25 Righteous Father! The world does not know you, but I know you, and these know that you sent me. 26 I made you known to them, and I will continue to do so, in order that the love you have for me may be in them, and so that I also may be in them.". (John 17:1-26)

Wow! Wasn't that powerful! You've read many biblical prayers and should have obtained some of the spirit of those prayers. Were you able to identify some of the protocols and elements of prayer in these prayers? Now, you have a prayer resource that you can reference anytime.

You should feel confident you can establish and maintain a vibrant prayer life. However, your practice of prayer must be a daily practice. The best way to develop this practice is to identify a specific place or location for your daily prayer. It can be one side of your bedroom, a study, or a walk-in closet. The idea is for you to identify a location that is intimate and available daily. Then, you choose a time to enter that location and practice the protocols and elements of prayer. The consistency of time and location is very effective for firmly establishing habits.

After you have become accustomed to spending time with God in prayer, you will see great results in your walk with God as your relationship with God deepens. This is what you want, especially in the days of your youth, because this will carry on through to your adulthood.

Knowing how to touch God in prayer as a young person will significantly reduce your vulnerability to the devil's wiles and make you a catalyst for revival in your church. You will know how to supplicate for your needs and intercede for others' needs. You become an all-around better Christian and a better youth.

To take it to the next level in prayer, you take what you learned about memorizing the WORD of God, the Bible, in the first section of this book and combine it with prayer. The combination of Bible and prayer is potent as you begin to pray the Bible. For example, your prayer includes portions of the Bible, "Thank you, Lord Jesus, for bearing in your own body all of our sins on the tree and blotting out the handwriting of ordinances that was against us and contrary to us,' etc. When you pray the bible like this, you are amening or agreeing with God and further ingraining the truth of God's WORD deeper into your heart.

If you can commit to working on these two things: (1) Prayer and (2) Bible reading during the days of your youth, there is no telling how much good you can and will accomplish on behalf of God! Here is what you should do: take the challenge. Do what you have read in this book and see if the results will be forthcoming, as we have indicated. You will not be disappointed, young person. The days of your youth are time-limited, and you have only time to journey through them. Make the best of this stage of your life, and your future will testify to your choices today.

Bible Reading Plan

In conclusion, this book has exposed you to the wisdom literature of the Book of Proverbs and beautiful Biblical prayers, but the Bible has so much more to offer you, young person. **The Bible is an education in itself!** Your love for the Bible and its author, God, will grow as you read its pages more.

Do you need help getting started reading the Bible? We've got you covered. The Bible reading plan below will help you read through the Bible's library of books in an interesting and purposeful manner.

Start with the most important and most easily understood part of the Bible, the New Testament gospel of our savior, Jesus Christ.

1. **Matthew**
2. **Mark**
3. **John**

Next, read Luke's gospel of Jesus Christ and the Acts of the Apostles in the New Testament to complete your survey of Jesus Christ and the founding of the New Testament Church. The Book of Acts is the most exciting book in the New Testament and is the authoritative history of God's plan of salvation!

4. **Luke**
5. **Acts**

Now back up and gain bible literacy by reading the Pentateuch (the first five books of the Old Testament) and learn the origin of the creation and its creator God.

6. **Genesis**
7. **Exodus**
8. **Leviticus**
9. **Numbers**
10. **Deuteronomy**

The rest of the books of the bible are listed in an order that allows you to alternate between the Old Testament to New Testaments. Or you can read the Bible straight through from this point.

11. Hebrews	34. Ecclesiastes	57. Haggai
12. Joshua	35. Titus	58. Lamentations
13. Romans	36. Daniel	59. Ezekiel
14. Judges	37. Philemon	60. Zechariah
15. 1 Corinthians	38. Hosea	61. Malachi
16. Ruth	39. James	62. Proverbs
17. 2 Corinthians	40. Joel	63. Song of Solomon
18. 1 Samuel	41. 1 Peter	64. 1 Chronicles
19. 2 Samuel	42. 2 Peter	65. 2 Chronicles
20. Galatians	43. Amos	66. Psalms
21. 1 Kings	44. 1 John	
22. 2 Kings	45. 2 John	
23. Ephesians	46. 3 John	
24. Ezra	47. Obadiah	
25. Philippians	48. Jude	
26. Nehemiah	49. Jonah	
27. Colossians	50. Revelation	
28. Esther	51. Micah	
29. 1 Timothy	52. Nahum	
30. 2 Timothy	53. Habakkuk	
31. Job	54. Isaiah	
32. 1 Thessalonians	55. Zephaniah	
33. 2 Thessalonians	56. Jeremiah	

"Read the Bible through 100 times! Memorize it once and pray it in"
Bishop Tommy Jackson

Acknowledgements

While I do not consider myself an author or a writer, I humbly acknowledge that I am a compiler of information and must rightly credit the sources that have inspired and influenced this work.

First and foremost, I acknowledge my Lord and Savior, Jesus Christ, who gave himself a sacrifice for me so that he might redeem me from all iniquity. My greatest inspiration is His life, teachings, death, burial, and resurrection.

I am deeply grateful to the many men of God who have deepened my faith and knowledge of Jesus Christ through their passionate preaching and teaching. First among these men are my pastor, Reverend Justin Jackson, and my bishop, Reverend Tommy Jackson, who first shared the truth of the gospel of Jesus Christ with me and, through many years of exceptional leadership and example, molded me by the Word of God into the man I am today.

I also want to express my heartfelt gratitude to my good friend, Pastor Ernest Stephens. His unwavering support and the opportunities he's provided over the years have deepened my love for youth ministry.

Of the many books I have read over the years on youth, the one that most informed and influenced this work is "The Teenage Brain" by Frances E. Jensen, MD, with Amy Ellis Nutt. I found it to be eye-opening and very helpful in understanding the cognitive and biological development of youth.

Lastly, the Holy Bible, the Word of God, has been and continues to be the most influential book in my life. This work includes excerpts from my favorite versions: the King James Version, and a blend of the Complete Jewish Bible, and Today's English Version.

Michael A. Angelle Sr.